Tricks
with
Chintz

By Nancy S. Breland

TRICKS
WITH
CHINTZ

Using Large Prints
To Add New Magic
To Traditional Quilt Blocks

American Quilter's Society

P. O. Box 3290 • Paducah, KY 42002-3290

Library of Congress Cataloging-in-Publication Data
Breland, Nancy S.
Tricks with Chintz: using large prints to add new magic to traditional quilt blocks/by Nancy S. Breland.
p. cm.
Includes bibliographical references.
ISBN 0-89145-834-4: $14.95
1. Patchwork – Patterns. 2. Quilting – Patterns. 3. Chintz.
I. Title.
TT835.B696 1994   93-47384
746.9'7 – dc20   CIP

Additional copies of this book may be ordered from:

American Quilter's Society
P.O. Box 3290
Paducah, KY 42002-3290

@$14.95. Add $1.00 for postage & handling.

Dedication

To Judy Weinrich, who has started so many of us on joyous quiltmaking journeys. She guides us, shares her pleasant company, and occasionally carries our bags.

Acknowledgments

I give grateful thanks to all of the Hopewell Valley Quilters, who have generously encouraged my growth as a quiltmaker. I want especially to thank Ellen Bell, who gave me my first quilting lesson and who continues to advise me not to end a project before it is really done.

Jay Turkel of Princeton Photographics, Inc. is the genius behind the camera who took photos of all quilts in this book.

PINWHEELS, 46" x 44", 1992. Pinwheel block,
pattern page 82. Machine pieced, hand quilted.

Table of Contents

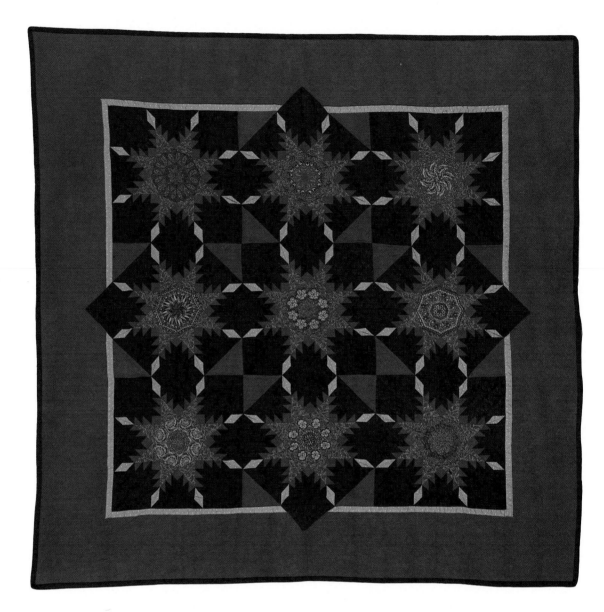

FEATHERED STAR, 57" x 57", 1988. Feathered Star block.
Machine pieced, hand quilted.

INTRODUCTION

Why is the quilt shown opposite so pleasing? Many people are fascinated by the patterns formed in the centers of the chintz blocks. These designs may remind them of those seen in kaleidoscopes, irresistible toys for people of any age.

Kaleidoscopes make images based on the principle of radial symmetry – designs repeat radiating around one central point. Many of our favorite patterns are based on this type of symmetry: petals of flowers, starfish, children's drawings of stars and the sun, a drop in a pool of water, pinwheels, and snowflakes. In quilts, similar types of designs can be created with fabric, particularly with large chintz prints.

Quiltmakers seem especially drawn to quilts combining chintz fabrics and blocks with radial symmetry because this design approach opens up all sorts of new possibilities. A flip through the illustrations in this book will show that many of the quilts are based on very simple blocks that can be pieced on the sewing machine.

Though the blocks are simple, they have the visual appeal of intricately appliquéd needlework because of the way chintz fabrics are used. Chintz fabric also allows quiltmakers to incorporate curved designs without having to piece curved seams, an activity sometimes religiously avoided by machine piecers.

Kaleidoscopes never fail to produce pleasing patterns. If you master the tricks of creating special effects with chintz, your quilt blocks will always make pleasing patterns, too.

Chapter 1
SELECTING CHINTZ FABRIC

To experiment with special effects with chintz, you'll probably have to expand your fabric collection. Just when you thought your fabric library was complete, you'll need to create a new category, and then search to fill it!

Most of the fabrics featured in quilts in this book would be referred to as "decorator chintz" in stores. *Chintz* is a term applied to a large print cotton fabric that is often glazed and usually printed with several colors. It is manufactured not for quiltmaking or dressmaking, but rather for use in home interiors for draperies or upholstery. A few large scale fabrics printed for quiltmaking or dressmaking may be appropriate for the projects in this book, but most of the prints commonly sold for quiltmaking are too simple in design and too small in scale to work well.

Decorator fabric is usually not sold with dressmaking fabric or in quilt shops. Decorator fabrics can often be found in one area of a multi-purpose fabric store, or in a store which specializes in fabrics for home interiors. Decorator fabric is usually printed in 60" widths, rather than the standard 45" for fabric used by most quiltmakers. Rather than being wrapped on bolts, this fabric is usually rolled on long cardboard tubes and displayed on racks.

Decorator fabric can be very expensive, as you realize if you have recently bought fabric for drapes. However, seconds and discontinued fabrics are often deeply discounted, and may be available on tables in flat folds. Seek out these lower priced fabrics. Even fabric with flaws can be used. You can work around stains and smears – and you will be less distressed when you "make lace" out of a piece of decorator fabric that you bought at a discount.

Not all fabric made for draperies and slipcovers is suitable for quiltmaking. You will need to search for fabric that is appropriate in both design and construction.

Select plain weave, medium-weight cottons.

Much of the fabric manufactured for interiors does not work well for quiltmaking. You'll want to limit your search to chintz that will combine with fabrics typically used for quilts. First, the fabric should be 100% cotton. Cotton has no memory, so it will stay where it's put and will hold a crease when pressed. Once it has been washed, it is soft to the hand. Stitches will nestle comfortably into the valley they create on the quilt's surface. On the other hand, fabric with polyester in it always wants to spring back – it won't take directions from you or from your quilting thread.

Sometimes, the fiber content of the fabric will not be known, especially if it is sold in flat folds. Fiber content of mystery fabric can be tested in a couple of ways. If the fabric is 100% cotton, it will wrinkle when wadded up in a corner. The loose fibers on the cut edge of the fabric will have a soft feel – not stiff or wiry. The surest test for cotton fabric is the burning test. In the fabric store, pull off just a few threads from the cut edge of the mystery piece. Take the threads outside of the store, twist them up and burn them with a match. Cotton fibers will burn with an even flame. Blow out the flame, and the smoke will smell good, usually, like burning leaves. Once the ash is cool, feel it. Cotton ash will be like powder – soft and small. If you burn some threads with polyester in them, you'll have a very different experience. The flame will burn unevenly, even furiously. (Watch your fingers!) The smoke will smell awful, like burning plastic. Blow out the flame, and after all is cool, feel the ash. It will be rough, like melted plastic.

The fabric you select for your quilt must also be appropriate in its weight and construction. You'll be using the decorator chintz alongside other fabrics, and you'll want them all to be compatible in weight. Decorator fabric is somewhat heavier than dress-weight goods, but is not so heavy that it won't work with the lighter goods. Remember, you'll have to quilt through the fabric, so if it is too heavy or dense you are unlikely to meet with success.

Avoid fabric that is not plain woven. Fabric that is twill or other weaves ravels very easily. Twill weave is characterized by subtle diagonal lines across the face of the fabric. Twill is often much heavier than the other fabrics you will be using. Blue jeans are twill weave – you can see little diagonal patterns on the surface of the fabric. Most quiltmakers would be justifiably reluctant to use blue-jean fabric for a quilt. Likewise, avoid decorator fabric that is woven like blue jeans, even if the print on the surface is beautiful.

Look for prints that are clear and varied.

Now that you have limited your search to fabric that is work-able in fiber content, weight, and weave, what sort of designs in the fabric should you look for? Great fabric for special effects is characterized by great printed lines and shapes. Usually we are drawn to fabric for its appealing color or attractive motifs. For these projects, however, you'll be isolating and repeating only a small portion of the pattern in the printed fabric. You might first be drawn, for instance, to a particular flower on a piece of fabric, but you must train yourself to look instead for lines and shapes in the fabric – a part of a petal or a particularly graceful stem, or an intriguing space between the motifs that you can use to create an interesting block.

Train yourself to shop for fabric with a window template in your mind – or in your hand. A window template made from an index card is illustrated in Fig. 1-1. Looking at a pattern on a piece of decorator chintz through the window will help you find exactly the part of the pattern you might like to use. Scan the fabric to see if it has interesting lines and shapes that can be used for your project. How will the fabric look when it is cut up and sewn together with identical pieces?

FIG. 1-1.
A window template placed over a piece of chintz
will help to isolate interesting shapes.

Some printed fabric is going to be disappointing because it has too little contrast. Soft pastels soothe, but won't have sufficient contrast in them to make a striking kaleidoscopic image. You'll be happier working with fabric in which the printed figures are very distinct from the background. "Cartoon prints," those which have each print motif outlined with a thin black line, make very crisp designs and can be used to make wonderful quilt blocks.

Some fabrics will be unsuitable because they appear fuzzy in

FIG. 1-2.
This fabric would be difficult to work with because the flowers and leaves are too closely spaced, and the outlines of the figures are not distinct.

FIG. 1-3.
This fabric would also be difficult to work with because the designs are not distinct.

their design. While the colors may be bold, the individual motifs may have ambiguous edges, blending softly into the background. Again, great as these fabrics may look on the bolt, they would be difficult to work with. You'll be cutting up motifs very precisely to make your quilt, and you'll have to be able to see the edges of each motif clearly so that the template can be placed accurately. If the printed image on the fabric is not distinctly "focused," it will be difficult to work with.

FIG. 1-4.
Even small shapes cut from this fabric would not produce interesting effects because the flowers are too small.

FIG. 1-5.
This print is too small in scale.

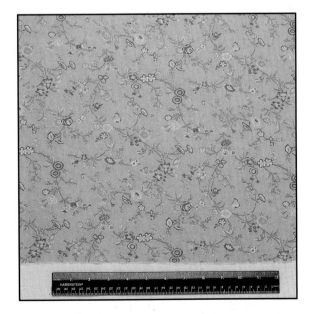

If you find a fabric with a stripe as well as areas without stripes, you have found a treasure! Stripes give great options when you are creating exciting centers in blocks. Sometimes fabric is printed with mirror images, where a floral pattern appears side by side with an identical but reversed image of that pattern. Mirror image prints open up even more design possibilities.

Look for fabric with a variety of motifs. A beautiful floral print

FIG. 1-6.
A single motif in the fabric limits the number of interesting "centers" you can create.

FIG. 1-7.
Fabric with many different motifs will work very well.

featuring just one rose, for instance, will not give very many options for different centers in blocks. A print with different roses, buds, leaves, and stems will be much more fun to work with. When reviewing fabrics, check not only the figures on the printed fabric, but also the shapes between the figures. Sometimes the shapes in the background can be used to make wonderful blocks.

FIG. 1-8.
This fabric is ideal.
It is large in scale, motifs are outlined with black, and the lines and shapes are interesting.

FIG. 1-9.
This fabric would be exciting to work with.
It is large in scale, and has interesting lines and shapes. It would make an interesting design if blocks were set into fabric that matched the background of this chintz.

FIG. 1-10.
A stripe is a bonus!
This is a great fabric.

Purchase enough fabric for your project.

You can't depend on simple yardage to determine how much chintz fabric you'll need to buy for your project. Instead, you'll have to count the number of times any motif on the printed fabric appears. In some very large print fabrics, the individual motifs repeat only occasionally. Look for repeats both down the selvage and across the width of the piece. Sometimes the designs will appear two or three or four times across the width of the fabric.

To make blocks based on Eight-Pointed Stars or octagon designs, you'll need a minimum of eight of each printed motif. Hexagon-based blocks will need just six, and patterns based on four right angles will need just four repeats. If you are going to work with Blazing Stars or variations of Lone Stars, you may want to buy enough fabric for 16 repeats.

Remember, when you cut a design out of fabric, you may interfere with your ability to use a motif nearby. Sometimes you will make mistakes, so you might want to buy a little more than the minimum you need. It is fun to use a piece of the uncut chintz in a border, so viewers can search for the original motif featured in the centers. If you are going to put a sleeve on the back of your quilt so you can hang it, consider making the sleeve out of the original uncut chintz. Buy all you need, and perhaps a little more.

You may be tempted to buy enough of the chintz to put it on the back of the quilt. While that might look great, it will be extraordinarily difficult to quilt. The fabric you have chosen is probably denser than fabric you typically use for quiltmaking, and hand quilting through it on the front and the back will be like quilting a tent! Unless you plan to machine quilt your finished project, choose some fabric for the back that is not quite so heavy.

After purchasing the piece of chintz, put it in the washer and dryer. This will, indeed, remove the glaze on the surface, but it will also shrink the fabric and make it compatible with the other fabrics you'll be using in your project. If you can't bear to sacrifice the glaze, plan never to wash your finished project.

Fabrics manufactured for drapes or slipcovers seldom if ever bleed in the wash. However, some manufacturers of dress-weight fabrics or fabrics for quiltmakers may produce large-scale prints that are not colorfast in the wash. Wash the fabrics first. It's always better to be safe than sorry. ■

FIG. 1-11.
TRIFLE, 33" x 33", 1990.
Castle Keep block variation. Machine pieced, hand quilted.

CHAPTER 2
PICKING
A BLOCK

A number of traditional quilt blocks, some of which are fairly obscure, will work very well for showcasing the special effects that can be achieved by precision cutting chintz. You'll notice that in the quilts featured in this book, chintz is used in the center of blocks, where identically shaped pieces come together. In effective blocks, the area where the pieces come together is usually a large portion of the total block.

Many blocks which are effective for working with chintz come from the eight-pointed star family: Eight-Pointed Star, Castle Walls, Feathered Star, Arkansas Star, Wheel of Fortune, Blazing Star, and variations of these blocks. However, the use of special effects does not need to be limited to blocks featuring eight identical diamonds or triangles in the center. The alternate blocks in SPRING GARDEN (opposite) are squares made from four identical triangles coming together. NIGHT SKY (page 22) has some figures made from simply four right triangles.

Choosing blocks with four or eight pieces in the center is a good idea for practical reasons: these blocks end up square. While

FIG. 2-1.
SPRING GARDEN, 65" x 92", 1988. Eight-
Pointed Star block (pattern page 76).
Machine pieced, hand quilted.

some setting in may need to be done, these blocks can still be sewn on the machine. The resulting square blocks can be combined easily with other square blocks, sashing, or other rectangular units.

Chintz can also be cut into identical equilateral triangles, and sewn so six come together to create the radial design.

FIG. 2-2.
NIGHT SKY, 54" x 44", 1990.
Eight-Pointed Star block (pattern pg. 76)
and Lone Star block.
Machine pieced, hand quilted.

JACK FROST (below) is an example of this pattern. The six pieces give a simple, but still effective radial design, and of course remind the viewer of snowflakes. However, using patterns based on a geometry of equilateral triangles offers more challenges for the machine piecer, who may not be comfortable piecing hexagons together.

Effective designs can be created with chintz using a great many blocks, some easy to piece and others more challenging. Choose a block that you can easily sew. The classic Eight-Pointed Star block, part of every sampler quilt curriculum, offers plenty of opportunities to explore tricks with chintz. ■

FIG. 2-3.
JACK FROST,
27" x 34", 1991.
 Hexagon Star block
(pattern pg. 80).
Machine pieced,
hand quilted.

CHAPTER 3
CHOOSING OTHER BLOCK FABRICS

Once you have found a piece of chintz and have chosen the block you want to use, you will need to select some fabrics to complete your project. What should you choose?

Colors.

First, keep in mind that the background and complementary fabrics you select should be simple, with no bold patterns. The fabric you want to feature in the quilt is the fabric you have already selected – it is the chintz. If you select additional fabrics that are large in scale and brightly colored or busy, they will detract from the chintz. To be effective, quilts featuring special effects with chintz should have only one "main player." Other fabrics should not compete with the chintz.

The hues to choose for the non-chintz components of your block and for the remainder of your project are easy to select. In most instances, the chintz is printed with several colors, and you only need to select from these the ones you like. If your chintz has blue in it and you choose blue for another part of the quilt, the blue in the chintz will dominate and the other hues will be less prominent. It is fun to hold your chintz against various fabrics to see how its character changes.

Two sets of quilts – SPRING GARDEN and WAVERLY RECON-STITUTED; RECONSTITUTION #1 and RECONSTITUTION #2 – show the differences the hues of complementary fabrics can make in the overall impression the quilt makes. The blocks in RECONSTI-TUTION #1 and RECONSTITUTION #2 are cut from the same piece of chintz. One is set with blue and rose, which bring out these hues in the chintz blocks. The other is set with green and a brighter, more intense rose, making these hues in the chintz more prominent. SPRING GARDEN (page 21) and WAVERLY RECONSTI-TUTED (page 26) are also cut from the same print, but the background coloring of the two pieces is not quite identical. As a result the finished pieces have emphasized different hues in the chintz.

FIG. 3-1A.
The hues of the other block fabrics selected can make a big difference in the overall impression the quilt makes.

ABOVE: RECONSTITUTION #1, 32" x 32", 1992. Lone Star pattern. Machine pieced, machine quilted.

ABOVE: RECONSTITUTION #2, 27" x 34", 1991. Eight-Pointed Star block, pattern page 76. Machine pieced, hand quilted.

FIG. 3-1B.
WAVERLY RECONSTITUTED,
 45" x 57", 1991. Eight-Pointed Star
block, pattern page 76.
Machine pieced, hand quilted.

Values.

The effectiveness of the overall design will depend on more than just the hues selected to go with chintz. The values of the complementary fabrics must also be varied. Our visual system is more tuned to differences in values (lightness to darkness) than it is to hue – we perceive shapes because the value of the figure is different from the value of the background. In designing a quilt, you want to emphasize the value differences between the shapes (chintz centers and blocks) and their background.

In all of the quilts in this book, there is a sharp value contrast between the figures and the background. In HIDDEN PICTURES (below) you see the stars (light value) against the background (dark

FIG. 3-2A.
Value contrast between the figures (chintz centers) and their background is essential for an effective overall design.

RIGHT: HIDDEN PICTURES, 41" x 56", Eight-Pointed Star block, pattern pg. 76. Machine pieced, hand quilted.

value). The central star in EMERALD STAR (below) is fairly dark, and it is set on a lighter tan background. It is the contrast in the values of the patterns, not the contrast in hue, that makes the geometric designs visually prominent.

Of course, background areas in a quilt can be interesting, yet sufficiently subdued if fabrics of different hues but similar values are chosen. CHRISTMAS STARS (page 29) has background pinwheel blocks in complementary colors (red and green), yet these reds and greens are generally similar in value. Because both hues are dark, the pinwheels do not themselves stand out. Instead, the much lighter

FIG. 3-2B.
It is contrast in values, not hues, that makes geometric designs stand out.

RIGHT: EMERALD STAR, 44" x 56", 1990. Simple Star variation in border, pattern page 84. Machine pieced, hand quilted.

JACK FROST, page 23, shows stars (dark value) against a background (light value).

star blocks and centers first catch the eye because they are different in value from the darker pieced background. The border stars in EMERALD STAR also illustrate contrast in value. These stars have red points on green blocks, but these areas are made from similarly dark muted fabrics, so the centers, rather than the stars, predominate.

FIG. 3-2C.
When blocks, like the pinwheels,
are made of fabric similar in value,
they do not stand out themselves.

ABOVE: CHRISTMAS STARS,
59" x 38", 1992. Wheel of Fortune
block, pattern page 88.
Machine pieced, machine quilted.

Consider the background of the chintz.

Chintz consists of bold figures printed on a background, and you can create some different effects by selecting either contrasting setting pieces or setting pieces that match the background. The chintz in HIDDEN PICTURES (page 27) and CHINTZ MEDALLION (below) is printed on a soft tan, and the stars are set into a sharply contrasting background. As a result, the shape of the star stands out.

In other quilts, the background of the chintz fabric does not contrast with the adjacent pieces. NIGHT SKY (page 22) is made from fabric that has a black background. The pieced stars and squares were set into black fabric. When the background of the chintz print matches the background of the block, the piecing lines will disappear and the printed design will appear to float on the background. The same technique is used in RECONSTITUTION #2 (below). The chintz has an off-white background. The simple Eight-Pointed Stars are set into a muslin background, and the seam lines

FIG. 3-3.
Different effects can be achieved by matching or not matching the background color in the chintz fabric.

ABOVE: RECONSTITUTION #2.

ABOVE: CHINTZ MEDALLION, 45" x 45", 1988. Carpenter's Wheel block (variation). Machine pieced, hand quilted.

disappear. If you want your symmetrical designs to "float," match the background fabric used in the block to the background color on the printed chintz.

A word of caution: don't get the two approaches – contrasting setting pieces and matching setting pieces – mixed up. If you have chosen a fabric to set your stars that contrasts with the background of the printed chintz, make certain that it does in all cases. In SPRING GARDEN, (page 21) the stars are set into a dark blue-green. The dark blue-green matches exactly the blue-green in the printed chintz. Fourteen of the stars look identical with sharp points against the green background. Look carefully for the fifteenth star, the one that looks as if the points have been chopped off. What happened? In cutting the centers, a piece of the green in the chintz just happened to fall at the outer tip of the diamond used to make the star. The green tip blends visually with the green used to set the stars, and the piecing line seems to have disappeared.

Other considerations.

Keep in mind when selecting accompanying fabrics that very light-weight or loosely woven fabrics are not going to mix well with most decorator chintz, which tends to be dense. While some variation in the weight of fabrics can be managed in any quilting project, fabrics with large differences may be hard to piece, may not lie flat, and may ripple or pucker.

As with the chintz, prewashing the fabrics is recommended. Some manufacturers do not produce colorfast fabrics, and the brilliant color you love may bleed into adjacent fabrics when you wash the fabric. Forget home remedies or special care precautions; don't use a fabric that bleeds. Your work is too important to risk it to inadequately manufactured goods.

Put your accompanying fabrics in the dryer to be sure they are fully shrunk. Since the fabrics you are combining with decorator fabrics may be dress-weight fabrics, the shrinkage may not be the same. If all fabrics are washed and dried before they are cut for patchwork, different rates of shrinkage won't put your quilt in future jeopardy.

CHAPTER 4
DESIGNING
YOUR PROJECT

Designing a project using chintz requires additional decisions. You already have a piece of chintz and perhaps an idea about the block you'd like to create and the colors you want to use, but you're not yet ready to cut and sew your project. You must decide how large your block will be, and then you can build the rest of the project around the block size and the number of blocks you'll create. Some of the projects in this book began with a set of pleasing blocks. Only after they were sewn were the set and the ultimate size of the project decided upon. Other projects began with a pre-planned design worked out completely on graph paper. And other projects just grew.

Determining block scale.

The overall effect of the centers of your blocks will depend on the way you match the scale of the printed fabric to the size of the piece you cut from it. Your finished block size, and perhaps the size of the finished project, will depend on decisions you make regarding the scale of the print and the effect you choose.

If your print is a large scale, and you cut small pieces from it, you can isolate interesting lines, shapes, or background areas, but you may not be able to feature an entire motif from the printed fabric. GOOD FORTUNE (opposite) illustrates this well. The red on tan fabric was extraordinarily large in scale. (See Fig. 4-1.) Because the

FIG. 4-1.
Intriguing effects can be achieved when very large print fabrics, like the one shown above, are cut into small pieces for a chintz block.

RIGHT: GOOD FORTUNE, 56" x 56", 1988. Wheel of Fortune block pattern page 88. Machine pieced, hand quilted.

print is very large and the cut piece is small, no single complete flower or petal will fit. As a result, the original figures are lost. Note the intriguing effects that result when small pieces are cut from a very large scale fabric.

Now look at HIDDEN PICTURES (page 27). In this quilt, the scale of the decorator chintz is fairly small. The original fabric is used in the wide border, so you can see where the centers came from. Here, many of the centers give wreath-like effects because I was able to fit an entire flower or leaf into the diamond that makes the star.

There is a limit, however, to how small the print can be before the special effects will be lost. Imagine cutting an Eight-Pointed star from a small traditional calico. The motifs are so small that any really interesting kaleidoscope effects could not be achieved unless the block were worked in true miniature.

The overall principle here is to find a good relationship between the scale of the print and the size of the pattern pieces you plan to cut from it. Remember, you'll have to piece the final project, and if your pieces are too tiny, you'll have a tough time. Also keep in mind that most decorator fabrics are a little heavier than traditional quilting fabric, so cutting and sewing very small pieces might be more of a challenge than you may want to handle.

Designing the rest of the project.

When you have decided what size blocks are the best for the effect you want, the rest of the quilt can be designed. The overall design can be simple or complex. Blocks can be set together with no sashing, as in GOOD FORTUNE (page 33). CASTLE WALLS (opposite) and RECONSTITUTION #2 (page 30) are blocks set with simple sashing and a plain border. HIDDEN PICTURES (page 27) has blocks set on point. Blocks can be set with complementary blocks, such as SPRING GARDEN (page 21) or CHRISTMAS STARS (page 29).

Other quilts in this book show more complex variations of block sizes, sets, and pieced borders. MAGIC CARPET (page 36) was inspired by pictures of Oriental rugs. EMERALD STAR (page 28)

FIG. 4-2.
CASTLE WALLS,
45" x 45", 1987.
Castle Walls block,
pattern pg. 74.
Machine pieced, hand
quilted.

and ISLAMIC TILES (page 37) began as ideas drawn from a book showing Islamic tile work. Special effects can be achieved with chintz using many different overall geometric designs adapted to many quilt designs.

In the annotated references at the back of this book are some publications to consult for overall quilt designs and settings for blocks.

FIG. 4-3.
BELOW: MAGIC CARPET,
68" x 42", 1989.
Castle Walls block,
pattern pg. 74.
Machine pieced,
hand quilted.

FIG. 4-4.
OPPOSITE: ISLAMIC TILES,
66" x 86", 1992.
Arkansas Star block,
pattern pg. 70. Machine
pieced, hand quilted.

CHAPTER 5
MAKING & USING
TEMPLATES

At last, you're ready to create special effects with chintz! Begin by making your template. You'll need template material that is semi-transparent. Most plastic template materials sold in quilt shops will work well. To be safe, place the template material over your chintz to be sure you can easily see the printed pattern in the fabric. Some material sold for templates may be too opaque for you to be able to see the fine details in the fabric.

Making the template.

Begin by placing the template plastic over the drafted pattern piece and trace the seam line exactly (exactly!) with a fine tip permanent marker. Precision throughout the marking and cutting of chintz is essential because any imprecision, even a small error, will cause the kaleidoscopic image to be distractingly irregular.

Next, mark the cutting line on your template, exactly ¼ inch from the seam line. Then cut out the template. Templates used to construct the parts of the block which are not made from chintz must also be constructed carefully.

The template for cutting the chintz needs additional reference markings that are used to line up isolated motifs in the chintz. These reference lines should also be made with a fine tip permanent marker. Additional markings on a diamond shaped template are shown in Fig. 5-1. The center line runs exactly from point to point. Each of the parallel reference lines is exactly perpendicular to this center line. It doesn't matter how far apart these parallel lines are drawn. You can always add a few more as you work if you feel you need more reference points.

Note that on the diamond, the parallel reference lines appear only on the lower half of the template. That is because lines BC and CD will become seam lines where chintz motifs touch. Seam lines AB and AD will be sewn to background pieces of the block. In this part of the block, chintz designs will be free in open space, not touching other chintz designs.

Fig. 5-2 shows a correctly marked template for a triangle, one of eight, that will make an octagon in the center of a block. Note that in an octagon, line AB and line BC are both seam lines where chintz motifs will touch. No part of the chintz will be free, surrounded by only background fabric.

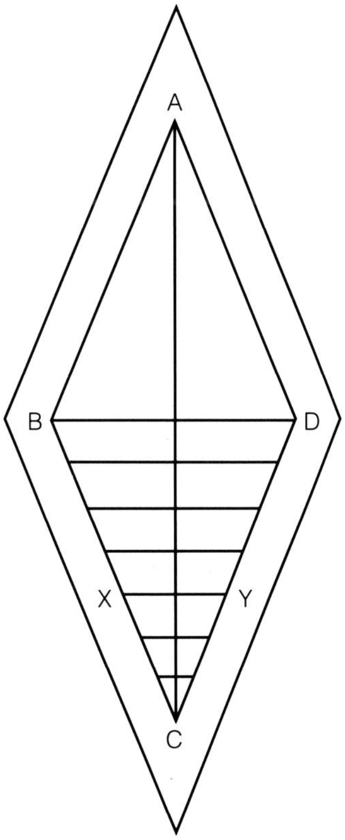

FIG. 5-1.
RIGHT: Reference markings on a diamond-shaped template.

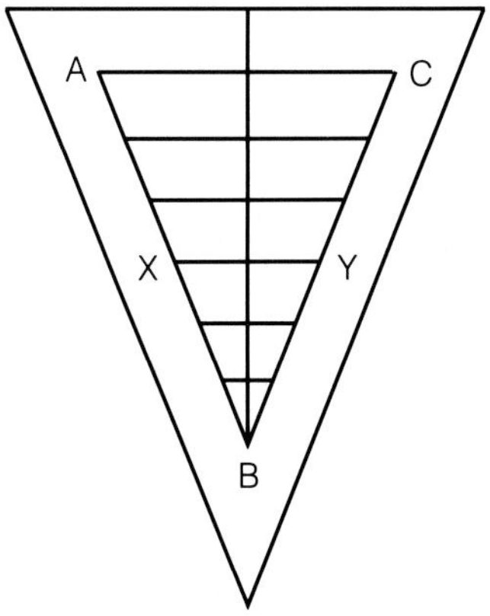

FIG. 5-2.
FAR RIGHT: Properly labeled triangle template.

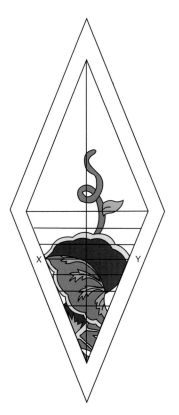

The parallel lines on these templates are reference guide lines used to show where two areas will match when sewn. The bit of the motif at point X (see Figs. 5-1 and 5-2) will be sewn to the bit of the motif at point Y. Sometimes you'll want to have a continuous line that goes around unbroken in the center of a star or octagon. If the template is placed so that the curve or straight line in the fabric crosses the seam line at point X and point Y, the sewn block will produce a visually unbroken pattern.

An example is shown in Fig. 5-3. Suppose this motif were isolated from the chintz. The edge of the figure at point X would also be the edge of the figure at point Y. When cut and sewn eight times, the shape shown in Fig. 5-4 would appear.

FIG. 5-3.

ABOVE: Position template so the curve or straight line in the fabric crosses the seam line at point X and point Y.

FIG. 5-4.

RIGHT: When the block is sewn, a visually unbroken pattern will be produced.

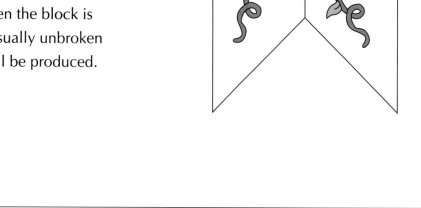

Using the template.

Once you have prepared the gridded template, the fun begins. Move the template around on your chintz and imagine what the centers are going to look like. Realize that you can't make a mistake, no matter what parts of the chintz you isolate and ultimately cut up. Did you ever see an ugly pattern through a kaleidoscope? Cutting up chintz is much like capturing an image in a kaleidoscope, with the exception that a kaleidoscope, made with mirrors, makes mirror images, and your quilt block will have identical images, with none reversed. Like a kaleidoscope, each image when sewn yields a delightful element of surprise. No matter how carefully you have planned your cuts, you can never imagine the exact image you will have until the last seam is sewn.

If at this point you are a little hesitant to begin to cut up your chintz fabric, try a just-for-fun practice run. Photocopy sections of your fabric. (Yes, expect raised eyebrows from onlookers!) Make enough copies of the original for the block you are working with (probably four, six, or eight). Prepare a special plastic template with just the seam lines (no cutting lines) to use with your photocopies. Mark and cut identical pieces from the photocopied fabric, and place them on plain paper. This photocopy exercise will produce an imitation of what the block will look like if actual cloth were cut and sewn. The photocopy has the additional advantage of being free of color so you can concentrate more easily on manipulating the shapes and lines in the printed fabric.

Keep in mind that you are searching for effective ways to use lines and spaces in the printed fabric. You may have chosen the fabric because you love a particular flower or butterfly, but try to put the objects themselves out of your mind. A tendril in the fabric needs to be seen as an interesting squiggled line. A petal or a leaf is a curve or a half circle. The space where a leaf and a stem meet creates a shape that can be repeated.

Hints for making good centers.

FIG. 5-5. EMERALD STAR (detail)

■ Match lines to create a continuous figure. The outside boundaries of these blocks are made by matching exactly the edges of the figure at the seam lines. The guidelines on the template will allow you to cut fabric so that, when sewn, lines will appear continuous.

FIG. 5-6. GOOD FORTUNE (detail)

■ Choose curves to give motion to your center. This block shows good motion. The curved leaf was isolated and cut in such a way that a spinning motif is made.

FIG. 5-7. GOOD FORTUNE (detail)

■ Use background spaces as well as figures. What look like petals of
the flower in the center of the block are made by matching points
of a thin leaf in the fabric. The matched points enclose white space
that joins to create each petal.

FIG. 5-8. GOOD FORTUNE (detail)

■ Cut circular printed motifs in half. This will create blocks reminis-
cent of fan blades, as shown in the block above.

FIG. 5-9. ISLAMIC TILES (detail)

■ When making octagons, create an outside border by choosing some motif that fits the base of the triangles which make the centers. This effect is shown in the block above.

FIG. 5-10. HIDDEN PICTURES (detail)

■ Create wreaths by capturing some background space in the middle of the block, as shown above.

FIG. 5-11. ISLAMIC TILES (detail)

- If the original printed fabric has a stripe, use the straight lines to create special effects.
- When the stripe matches exactly at the seam lines, smaller octagons appear, as shown in the block above.

FIG. 5-12. ISLAMIC TILES (detail)

■ Cut stripes so that they do not line up at the seam lines. Fans and Pinwheels result, as shown in the block above.

FIG. 5-13. RECONSTITUTION #2

■ When the chintz has a colored background and is set into fabric matching that background, other special effects can be created.

■ Cut the motifs so that the outer seam lines of the stars leave only the background of the fabric showing – no motifs touch the seam lines. This will give the effect of erasing the seam lines. The remaining figures will appear to float in the quilt, as they do in the quilt above.

FIG. 5-14. NIGHT SKY (detail)

■ Select just a little of a motif to fill the point of the star, as shown above in the block that features a green star with red points.

FIG. 5-15. SPRING GARDEN (detail)

■ When creating images out of four right triangles, look for curves in the chintz. Cut right, the curves will seam together to create a circular design, as shown above.

FIG. 5-16. SPRING GARDEN (detail)

■ When creating images out of four right triangles, images with straight lines will make squares or diamonds, as shown above and in NIGHT SKY, page 22.

What to avoid when making chintz centers.

While all patterns will be pleasing if cut and sewn precisely, some will be more pleasing than others. Here are some cuts to avoid. They are illustrated with some "duds" pictured on the following pages.

FIG. 5-17.

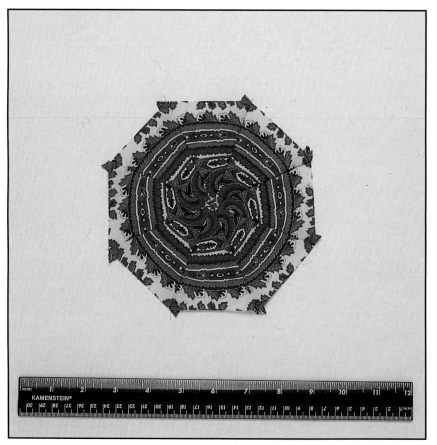

■ Adjacent pieces cut or sewn just a little "off," as shown above. If some of your lines meet at the seam line and others do not, if a little bit of a motif peeks out of some seam lines and not others, or if the pieces are askew, the magic of the kaleidoscopic effect is lost. It is difficult to rip and sew to correct a piece that has been cut just a little differently from the others. With attention to accuracy in cutting and sewing you can avoid these problems.

FIG. 5-18.

■ A tiny bit of a motif in the center can present problems, as shown above. It is very difficult to get small details to meet exactly in the very center when eight pieces meet. It is better to position the template so that the fabric falling in the exact center is a solid area, a background area, or some other area where lines are not distinct.

FIG. 5-19.

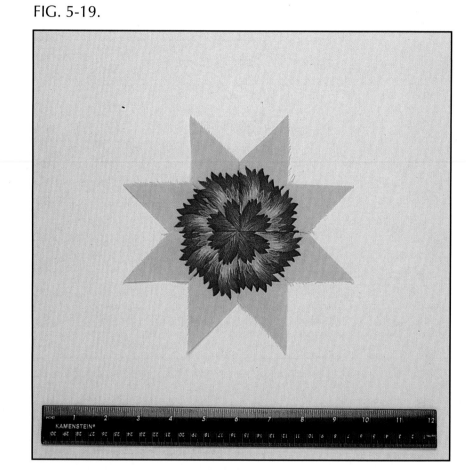

■ Re-creating a design already in the printed fabric. Suppose your chintz has a large chrysanthemum. You can cut a wedge from it, sew eight identical wedges together, and you've re-created the original flower, as above! If you have a radially symmetrical design in the chintz, to create a new and different design, cut it off-center.

FIG. 5-20.

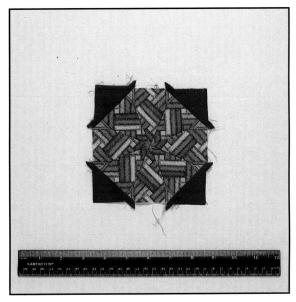

FIG. 5-21.

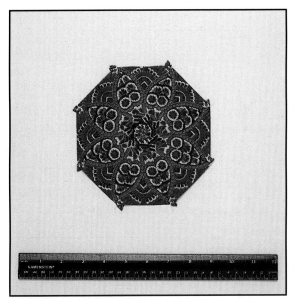

■ Creating too simple or too busy a design. You'll want some variety in line, color, or shading in each center you create. Repeating one simple leaf or flower and using a lot of background will make a less than exciting block. On the other hand, if your template is entirely full of pattern, the resulting block will be too busy like the blocks shown above. You need to select your cuts so that there is someplace for the eye to rest. You need to be able to see a figure as distinct from the background.

FIG. 5-22.

■ Motifs blending in with the setting fabric pieces. If a chintz motif touching an outer seam line matches with the adjacent, non-chintz piece of the block, the pattern seems to escape into the background territory. (See the discussion of this effect on pages 30 and 31.) Bland blocks like the one shown above, where the motif lacks good contrast with the background on which it is printed, should also be avoided.

Actually cutting the pieces.

When you've found a placement for your template, you're ready to cut chintz pieces. With a pencil, trace several parts of the chintz on to the template. Then cut carefully around the template. (A rotary cutter will produce cuts with the greatest accuracy, and is recommended. Marking seam lines with a pencil may stretch or distort the fabric a little so that you cannot maintain perfect accuracy.)

Then move the template to the same motif elsewhere on the fabric. Place the template exactly, matching your pencil lines to the fabric lines. Cut as many identical shapes as you need. When you have cut enough pieces for one block, you can then erase the pencil marks and use the template again and again to cut more centers for your blocks.

Many different blocks can be cut from one piece of chintz. Often the last blocks you make are the most interesting. When all of the obvious motifs are cut out, you are forced to consider more subtle leftovers. In the end, you'll end up

with a piece of chintz "lace," like that shown above. Indeed, this is not an efficient way to use fabric!

You probably realize that in cutting the pieces from the chintz, you have ignored the grain line. You have to do that because the effectiveness of your centers is dependent on your placing the template a particular way on the motifs in the printed pattern of the fabric. As a result, the "centers" you cut will be very unstable until they are sewn to background pieces, which you are able to cut following the rules for grain lines.

CHAPTER 6
PIECING THE CHINTZ BLOCKS

Accurate piecing is essential when you are creating special effects with chintz. Even if you have exactly cut identical motifs from fabric, errors in sewing will prevent the motifs from matching perfectly at each seam line. Inaccurate sewing will cause your center to remind you of the view in a cheap kaleidoscope with mirrors askew.

If you haven't recently pieced the block you have selected, it would be wise to do a practice block with scraps of fabric. Once you are confident, you can begin constructing your chintz blocks.

Begin by checking that your sewing machine will make exact ¼" seams. If your presser foot does not provide a very accurate guide, place a piece of tape on the soleplate exactly ¼" from the needle. The edge of this tape will be your guideline. Check the accuracy of your guideline by sewing on a sheet of four-squares-to-the-inch graph paper. Cut the edge of the paper along one of the printed lines. Place the cut edge of the graph paper along the guideline you have made, and sew. The perforations made by the needle should fall on the next printed line of the graph paper. If the stitches are even a little out of line, reposition your tape until the needle hits exactly ¼" from the tape.

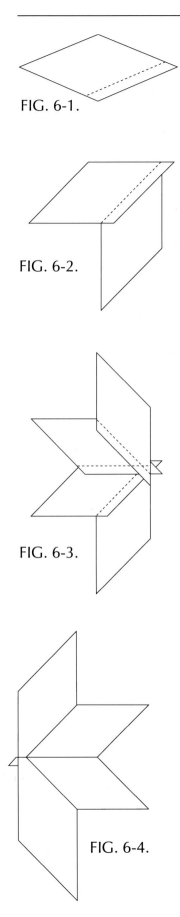

FIG. 6-1.

FIG. 6-2.

FIG. 6-3.

FIG. 6-4.

Piecing the chintz center.

Illustrations are given for piecing an Eight-Pointed Star. The same techniques can be used for piecing octagons, which are simply half diamonds.

Begin by sewing the eight cut diamonds in pairs. Place right sides together exactly, as in Fig. 6-1. The four pairs can be stitched one right after the next, without machine threads being cut in between them. When the seams have been sewn, cut the pairs of diamonds apart and the back of each will look like Fig. 6-2. Unfold each sewn unit and look at the front. Check that all four units look identical. If a matched line touches another printed line at the seam, be sure that each pair has an exact match. If a little bit of a motif peeks out of a seam line, be sure that bit is the same on each of the four units. Rip out and resew any seams that are inaccurate. Handle these pieces gently, especially when removing stitches. Remember that one or both edges are bias cut and will easily stretch if handled at all roughly.

Next, sew two pairs together to make half a block. The back of this half block will look like Fig. 6-3. Note that two seam lines cross. That intersection should be exactly ¼" from the edge of the block. Fig. 6-4 shows what the front of the block will look like. Again, be sure that all motifs match identically along the seam lines. Note also that the three seam lines meet exactly at one point.

Now prepare to sew the two halves together. Gently finger press the seams down on the top unit and up on the bottom unit. This will distribute the bulk at the point where the seams come together, and butting the units against each other will help with sewing accuracy.

Put the right sides together. Insert a positioning pin (perpendicular to the fabric) right through the center of the "x" in the seam line. Check the right side to see that the pin point comes out at the exact seam intersection on the right side of the unit. Then put the pin point through the right side of the bottom unit, exactly at the seam intersection. Check that the pin comes out exactly at the "x" on the underside of the piece.

Use the positioning pin as a spindle to press together the two

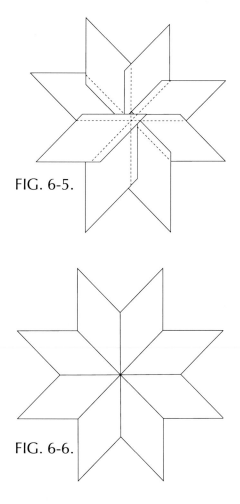

FIG. 6-5.

FIG. 6-6.

halves of the star. Pinch the pieces together with the pin perpendicular. Line up the rest of the edges of the units. Then about ½" above the positioning pin along the intended seam line, place a pin to actually hold the units together.

Begin to sew the seam, keeping both pins in place. Stop right before the first pin. Press your index finger down, fingernail right at the base of the positioning pin. This finger will hold the center as you sew. Don't let go! Remove both pins and carefully sew up to your fingernail. Then, one stitch at a time, go through the "x." Stop to align the lower half of the block. Hold it in place as you sew to the end.

Open your block. Isn't that center a wonderful surprise? Again, check that all printed lines on the fabric touch at the seam lines in the same way. This last seam is the toughest one. If you have any inaccuracies, gently rip and resew. Figs. 6-5 and 6-6 show how the back and front of the star block will look at this point in the construction.

Next, you'll be setting in the squares and the triangles to complete the block. Do not iron the center before you have completed the entire block. Remember that in cutting pieces from the chintz, you have ignored grain line. The star is very fragile, and ironing it now will distort it.

Completing the chintz block.

Complete the block with the squares. First, place a pin in the corner of the wrong side of the square, exactly ¼" from each edge. (You might want to put a pencil dot at this place.) Put a positioning pin in this spot. Then put the point of the pin in the seam line of the star, exactly where the new seam line will meet the previously sewn seam line. (See Fig. 6-7.) Line up the rest of the square, using the positioning pin as a spindle. Note that the little tip of the star ducks behind the square exactly ¼" from the edge of the square. As before, pin the two pieces together right above the positioning pin. Sew up to the pin, then put your fingernail down against the spindle. Remove both pins, and sew just to the spot where the spindle

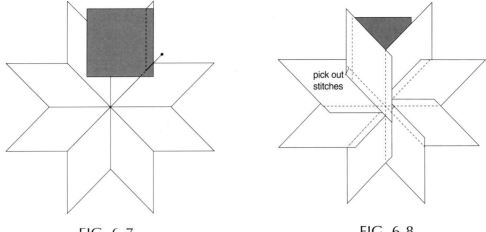

FIG. 6-7.

FIG. 6-8.

pin was. Then take a back stitch. Stop. Figs. 6-8 shows what the seam line looks like from the underside of the block.

Now, pick out the two or three stitches in the star unit that extend beyond your new seam line. This will free up the last ¼" of that seam line, so that you can set in the rest of the square.

Pivot the square so that its right side is along the second arm of the star where it belongs. Gently pinch the spot at the intersection so that it will lie flat. Put the block in your machine and put down the needle exactly where the previously sewn seam line ended. Position the square so that it lines up with the edge of the star arm. Sew from the seam intersection to the point of the star. Figs. 6-9 and 6-10 show how the block will look.

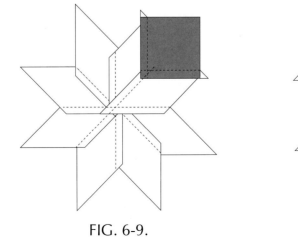

FIG. 6-9.

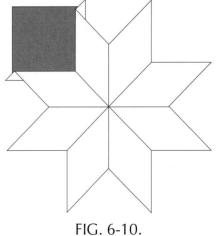

FIG. 6-10.

Set in the remaining three squares this way. Then use the same procedure to set in the triangles.

When you are all done, check that the points of each star stop ¼" from the edge of the block. If they are too close to the edge, you'll cut off the points when you sew the blocks to adjacent pieces. If the points are too far down, your block will be too small. Correct inaccuracies.

Notes on piecing other blocks.

Piecing diagrams for other blocks have been given at the end of this book. When piecing any block you will find that the use of a positioning pin at each seam intersection gives good accuracy.

The trickiest block to sew by machine is probably Castle Walls, because so many of the pieces must be set in. I recommend that the central octagon be made separately from the surrounding ring. The octagon is set in, one seam at a time, to the surrounding ring. Before attempting to set in the center, examine the underside of the completed ring. Check the "x" at the tip of each diamond which touches the center octagon. Be sure that it is ¼" from the edge, and that the seams are neither too wide or too narrow. Success requires that the base of the square match exactly the base of the triangle in the octagon unit. If one is longer than the other, the octagon will not set in neatly. Readjust the pieces so that the edges to be sewn together will be the exact same length. Then remove the two or three stitches (¼") from the seams of the octagon. Lay the octagon on top of the ring, right sides together. Put in the positioning pin through the "x's" and the octagon seam line. Sew "x" to "x" eight times.

Making a full quilt.

The pieced blocks you have made need to be put together into a quilt or wallhanging. Effective sets for chintz blocks can be simple or complex.

The simplest way to show the blocks is to set them together

with or without sashing. In GOOD FORTUNE, page 33, blocks are set together with no sashing, and a plain border is added around them. CASTLE WALLS, page 35, is almost as simple, with sashing and a matching border. The setting of blocks in RECONSTITUTION #2, page 25, is a bit more complex. In HIDDEN PICTURES, page 27, blocks are set on point, and separated with sashing cut from a simple stripe. In all of these quilts, decisions about how to set the blocks were made after the blocks were pieced. You might want to proceed this way. See how many different and pleasing blocks you can extract from a piece of chintz. Stop when no more can be cut, and then design the rest of your project.

Chintz blocks are also effective in more complex pieces. ISLAMIC TILES, page 37, MAGIC CARPET, page 36, and EMERALD STAR, page 28, were all planned and drafted on graph paper before any fabric was cut. If you enjoy the challenge of drafting and sewing complex projects, work this way.

The success of chintz quilts does not require complex design or difficult piecing. The radial symmetry in the block centers will draw the viewer's interest.

CHAPTER 7
QUILTING THE
PIECED QUILT TOP

From centers to blocks to a whole quilt top – the first part of your project is complete. How can you enhance the appearance of your top with your quilting design? As with any quilt, the quilting designs chosen must complement the design decisions you have made when piecing your top. Quilts featuring chintz fabric open up some new opportunities for quilting design.

First, decide how to use quilting lines to enhance the block centers. For large blocks and large chintz elements, quilting around the motifs you have created would be a good choice. Quilting around the dominant parts of the radial design you have created helps emphasize the figure and draws the eye away from the seam lines used to create the special effects. Sometimes your center will have fairly smooth continuous lines that stand out even more if the quilting stitches follow the outline. Smaller motifs, like a bud or a leaf, can be quilted around their periphery. This will make the motif puff out attractively.

You'll experience some technical difficulty, however, as you try to hand quilt in the very center of a block that has six or eight pieces of fabric coming together. Of course, you'll have clipped the excess fabric in the very center to help this part lie flat, but there's no getting around it: the center is very thick. Any heavier decorator fabric you have used adds to the thickness. Sometimes you must use a stab stitch to get through the absolute center. If you don't do some quilting near the center, you'll be left with a rather unattractive bubble. You might want to take just a few stab stitches to anchor down the very center of your block.

Quilting around chintz motifs, however, is not always the best idea for chintz quilts. In some centers, a single motif might not be obvious. The chintz fabric may be fairly busy with closely packed elements, or motifs may be too small to quilt around any one effectively. The centers themselves may be too small to outline much of anything. Small centers will have very little area that is thin and open – much of the center will be filled with seam allowances, making the area very hard to quilt through. It might be better in these cases to select a quilting line that emphasizes the radial nature of your block. Run a line of quilting stitches from the absolute center to the outside of the block or to the outside of the central area – much like the rays of the sun. While a line of stitching through any motif will distort it somewhat, the overall effect can be most pleasing. Also, a ray down the center of a triangle misses most of the seam allowances, which makes it technically easier to do.

Stitching block centers "in the ditch" is not recommended. This would emphasize the seam lines, and would counter the kaleidoscope effect you have created.

For the non-chintz parts of your blocks, choose quilting lines that will emphasize the simple geometric shapes. In the Wheel of Fortune block, for example, you might want to quilt in the ditch around the points of the stars. Or, you might want to stitch just ¼" inside the background pieces so that the points of the stars puff out against the background. If you stitched just inside the star points, you would flatten out the star, and the background would puff out. This may not be the look you like. Remember, you want your quilting design to emphasize the figures and to downplay the backgrounds in your blocks.

Quilting the rest of your project depends on the areas you have to work on. If you have created a piece with lots of open space, such as EMERALD STAR (page 28), you have space to do fancy work and background quilting. A plain border gives you space for elaborate fancy work. Since chintz fabrics are full of lovely curves, you can repeat the curved ideas in these open areas. Feathers in open areas complement lacy floral centers very effectively. You might even create a quilting design inspired by some of the specific elements in the chintz.

You may have chosen to include a border on your top made of the original chintz. If the elements in the chintz are large enough, you can quilt these borders by quilting around the printed motifs. This will give the effect of a lovely brocade. The outer border of EMERALD STAR is done this way. The border is made from a stripe in the original chintz. Quilting the individual flowers and leaves almost gives the appearance of an appliquéd border. Fool the eye!

If your quilt top has some very thin borders in it (an inch or less), quilting along the borders "in the ditch" or just outside the border is a good idea. This will help keep these lines crisp and straight. Quilting lines that intersect with a thin border tend to distort it, and just a small amount of distortion is very obvious on a narrow line.

As with any quilt, you'll want to be sure that your quilt is fairly evenly quilted throughout. If the middle of your quilt is very densely quilted and the borders are sparsely worked, your quilt won't lie flat.

Pattern Section

BLOCK

PATTERNS

On the next few pages are pattern pieces for many of the blocks shown in quilts in this book. At the top of each page is a picture of the block, shaded simply. Realize that you can vary the coloration any way you please to change the impact of the block. The white area of each block diagram is the area where you will put the identical chintz pieces.

Patterns for each block are given in various sizes, so you can choose the one that fits the scale of the chintz you have bought. Be sure to read the section in Chapter 4 on scale. You might want to trace out (on tracing paper) the template you plan to use for the chintz. Place the traced piece over the chintz to check the scale. If the template seems too small for the chintz, choose a larger size block or choose a different block with a larger area for the chintz. If your chintz is fairly small in scale, you may want to select a template that is smaller also.

Note that all patterns are drafted without seam allowances. You will need to add ¼" seam allowance to each pattern piece.

ARKANSAS STAR

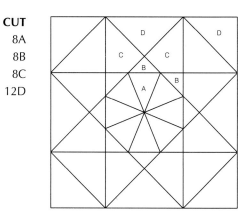

CUT
8A
8B
8C
12D

PIECING ASSEMBLY

- Sew 8 A pieces together to make an octagon.
- Sew 4 B pieces to the A unit to make a square.
- Sew D to C and B to C; then sew these triangles together to make rectangular unit. Make 4 units.
- Sew 2 D's together to make the square in the corner of the block. Make 4 units.
- Assemble units into 3 rows.
- Sew the 3 rows to complete block.

FULL-SIZE TEMPLATES
8" BLOCK
Add seam allowances.

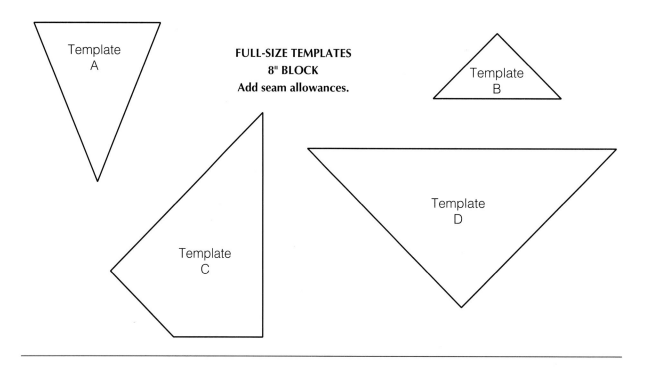

Template A

Template B

Template C

Template D

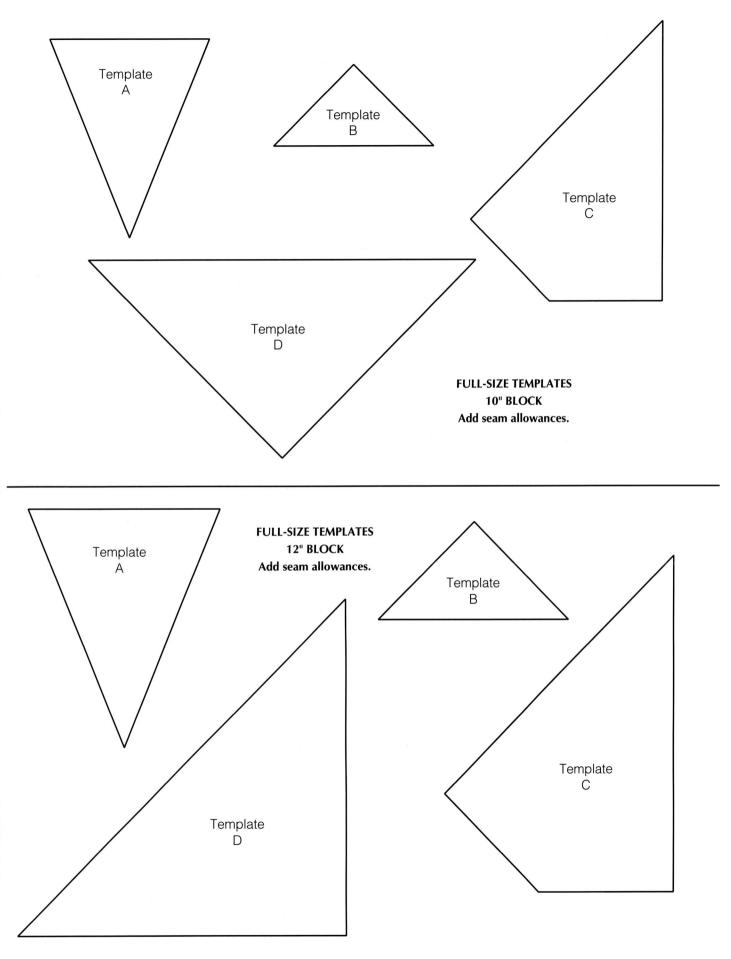

Template
A

Template
B

Template
C

Template
D

FULL-SIZE TEMPLATES
10" BLOCK
Add seam allowances.

FULL-SIZE TEMPLATES
12" BLOCK
Add seam allowances.

Template
A

Template
B

Template
C

Template
D

BLAZING STAR

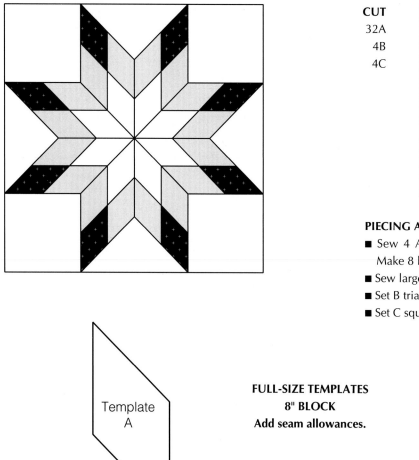

CUT
32A
4B
4C

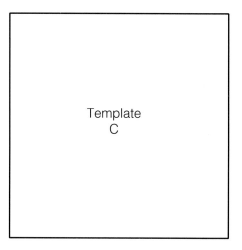

PIECING ASSEMBLY

- Sew 4 A diamonds to make a large diamond. Make 8 large diamonds.
- Sew large diamonds together to complete star.
- Set B triangles into star.
- Set C squares into star.

FULL-SIZE TEMPLATES
8" BLOCK
Add seam allowances.

Template
A

Template
B

Template
C

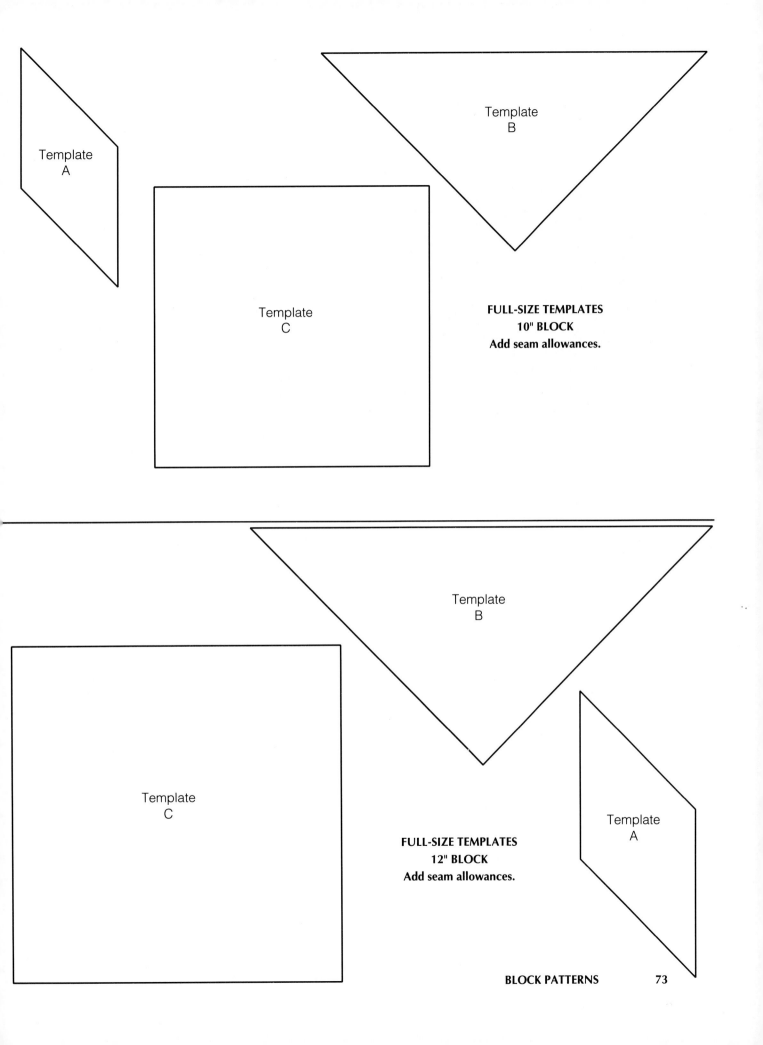

Template
A

Template
B

Template
C

FULL-SIZE TEMPLATES
10" BLOCK
Add seam allowances.

Template
B

Template
C

Template
A

FULL-SIZE TEMPLATES
12" BLOCK
Add seam allowances.

CASTLE WALLS

CUT
8A
8B
8C
8D
4E

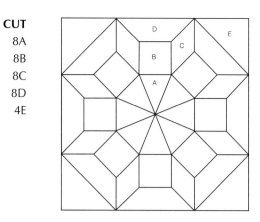

PIECING ASSEMBLY

- Sew pairs of A triangles together to make complete octagon.
- Sew B to D pieces.
- Set C to B-D unit.
- Sew BCD units together to make a ring.
- Sew E to ring.
- Set A octagon into B-C-D-E unit.

See piecing instructions on page 64.

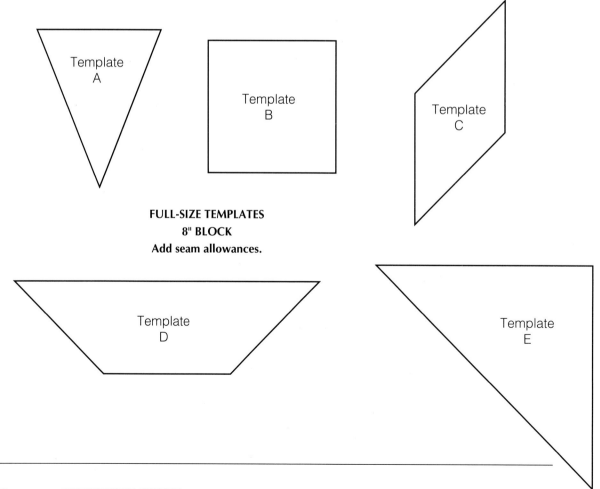

Template
A

Template
B

Template
C

FULL-SIZE TEMPLATES
8" BLOCK
Add seam allowances.

Template
D

Template
E

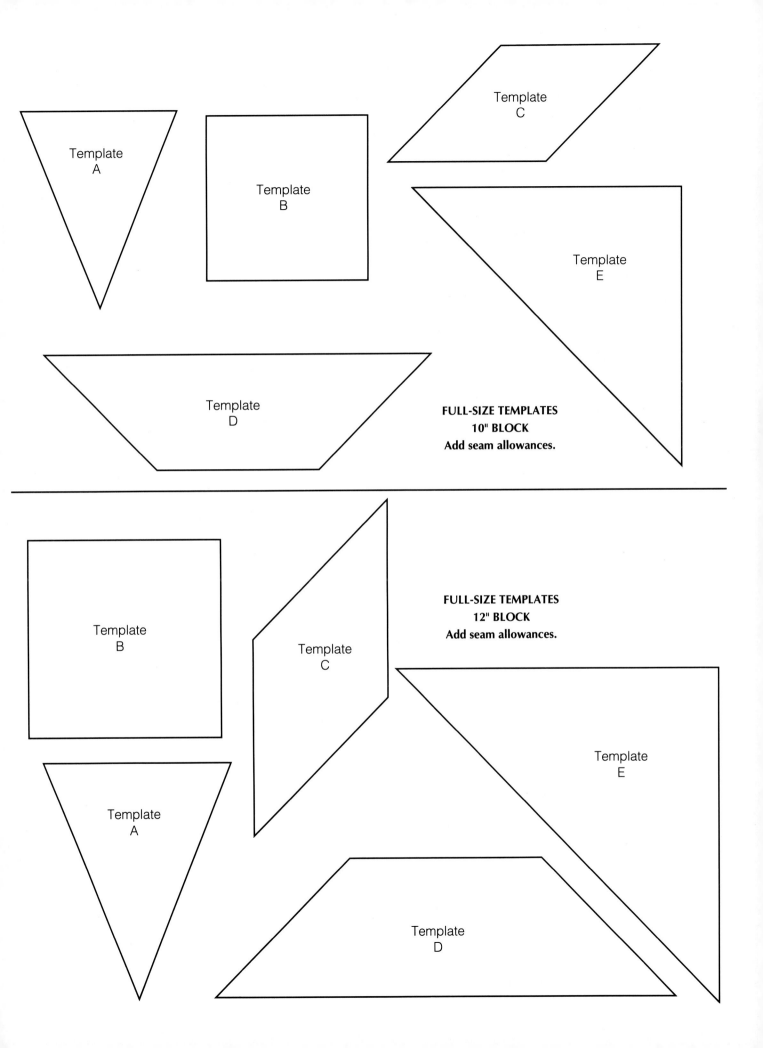

Template
A

Template
B

Template
C

Template
E

Template
D

FULL-SIZE TEMPLATES
10" BLOCK
Add seam allowances.

Template
B

FULL-SIZE TEMPLATES
12" BLOCK
Add seam allowances.

Template
C

Template
E

Template
A

Template
D

EIGHT-POINTED STAR

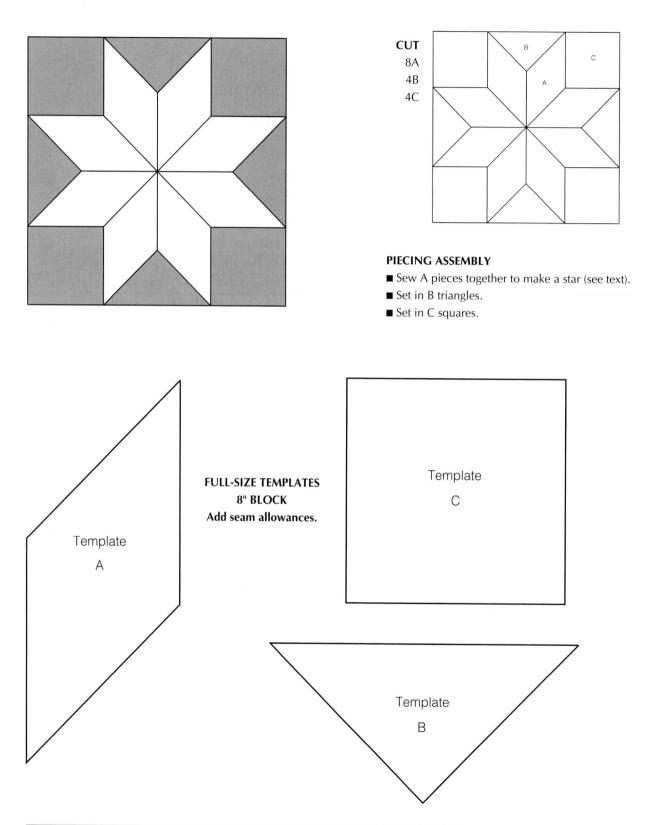

CUT
8A
4B
4C

PIECING ASSEMBLY
- Sew A pieces together to make a star (see text).
- Set in B triangles.
- Set in C squares.

FULL-SIZE TEMPLATES
8" BLOCK
Add seam allowances.

Template
A

Template
C

Template
B

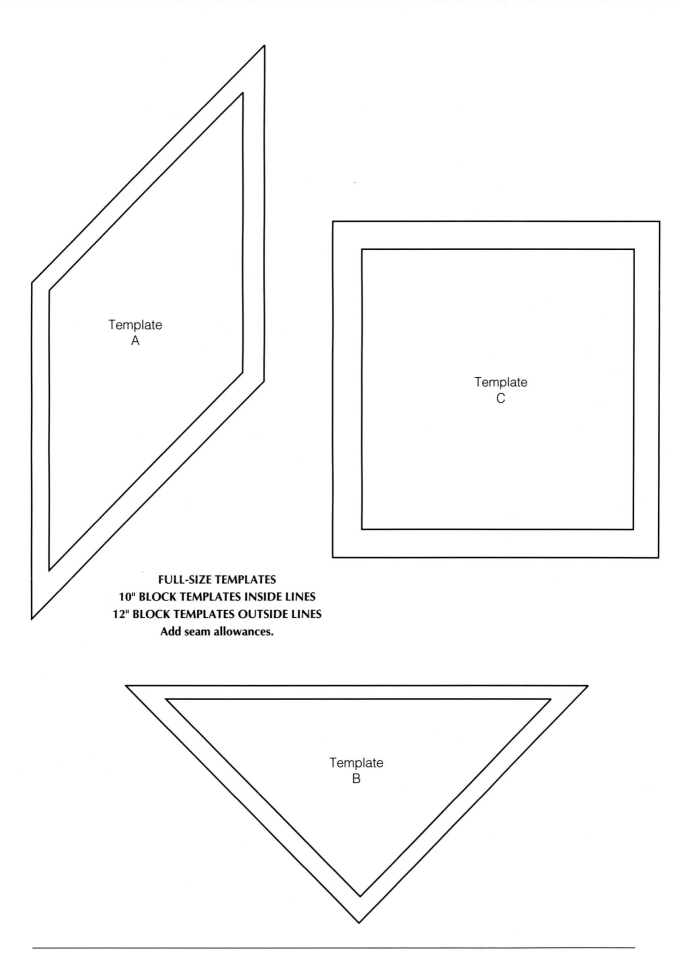

Template
A

Template
C

FULL-SIZE TEMPLATES
10" BLOCK TEMPLATES INSIDE LINES
12" BLOCK TEMPLATES OUTSIDE LINES
Add seam allowances.

Template
B

EIGHT-POINTED STAR VARIATION

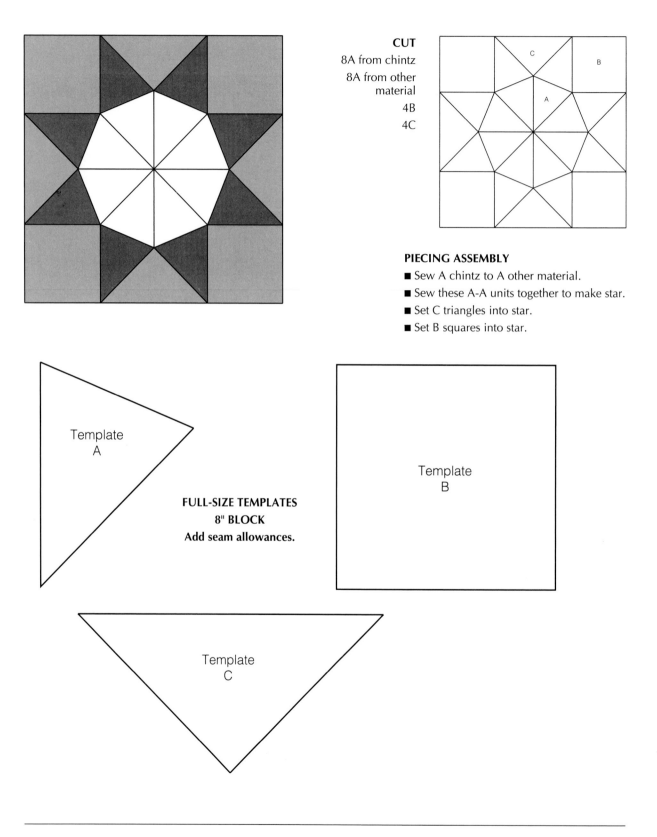

CUT
8A from chintz
8A from other
material
4B
4C

PIECING ASSEMBLY
- Sew A chintz to A other material.
- Sew these A-A units together to make star.
- Set C triangles into star.
- Set B squares into star.

Template
A

Template
B

FULL-SIZE TEMPLATES
8" BLOCK
Add seam allowances.

Template
C

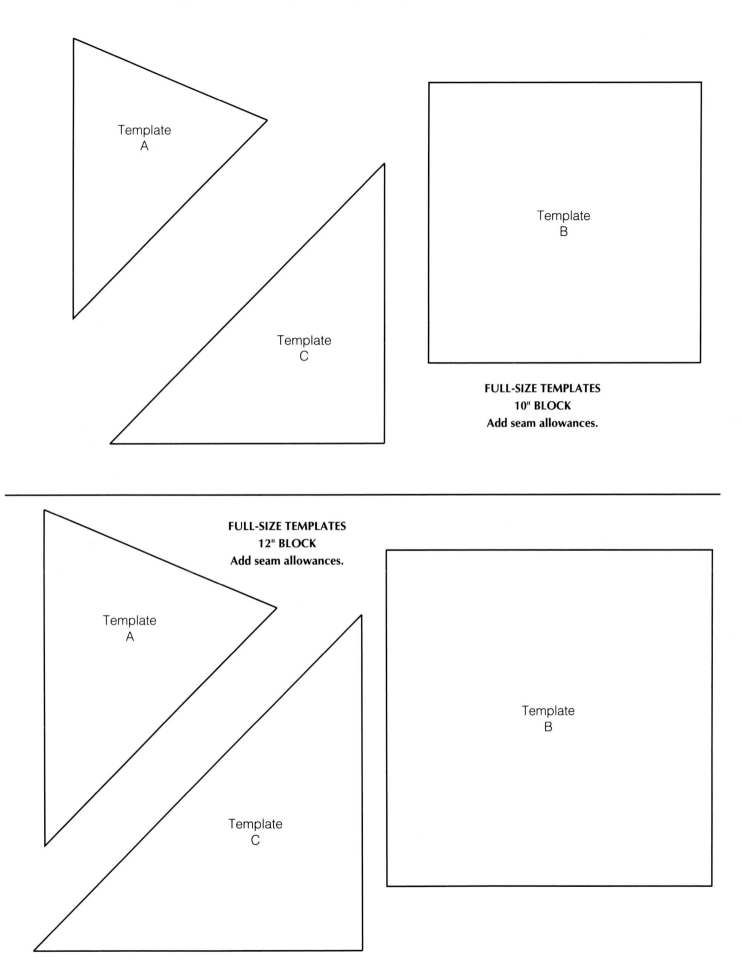

Template
A

Template
C

Template
B

FULL-SIZE TEMPLATES
10" BLOCK
Add seam allowances.

FULL-SIZE TEMPLATES
12" BLOCK
Add seam allowances.

Template
A

Template
C

Template
B

BLOCK PATTERNS   79

HEXAGON STAR

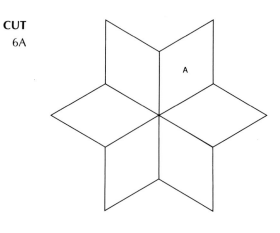

PIECING ASSEMBLY
- Sew 6 A blocks together.
- Sew to other pieces in your project.

FULL-SIZE TEMPLATE
SMALL STAR
Add seam allowances.

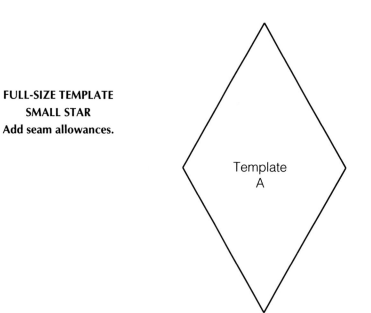

Template
A

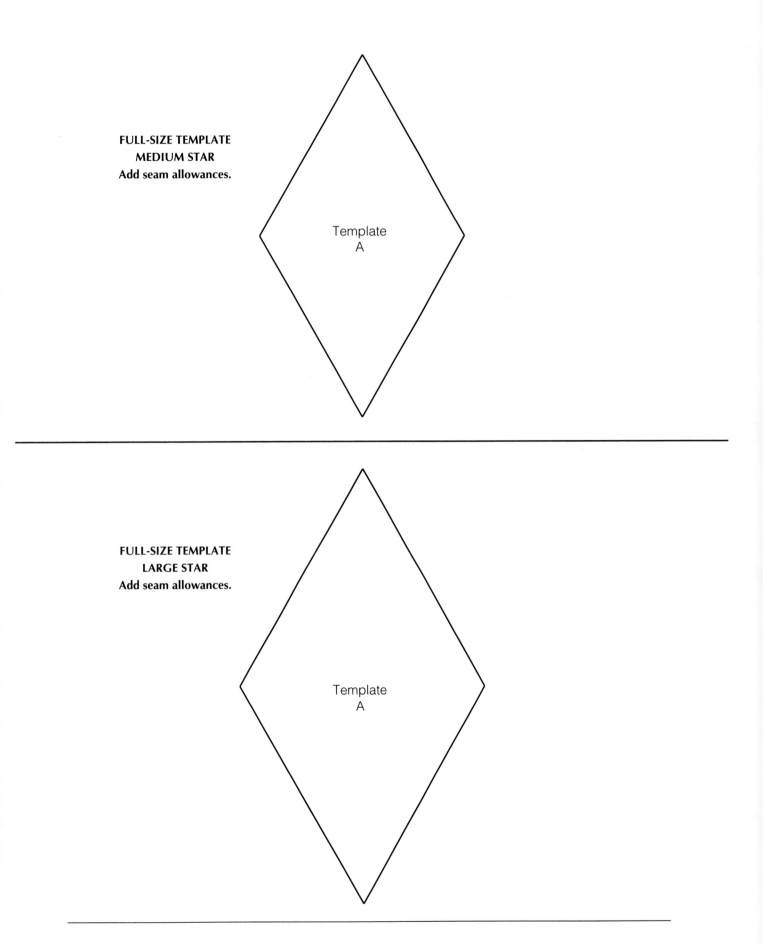

FULL-SIZE TEMPLATE
MEDIUM STAR
Add seam allowances.

Template
A

FULL-SIZE TEMPLATE
LARGE STAR
Add seam allowances.

Template
A

PINWHEEL

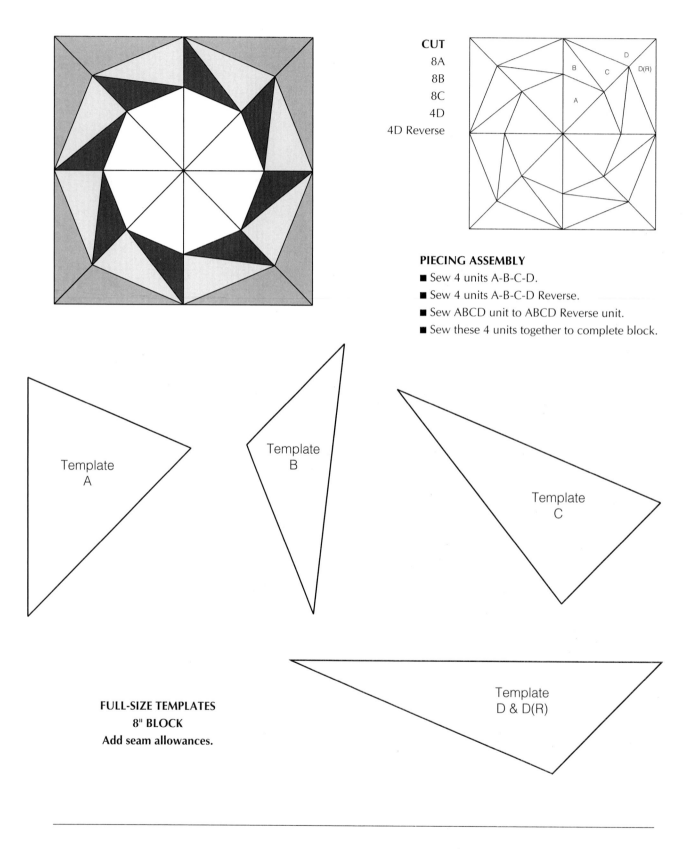

CUT
8A
8B
8C
4D
4D Reverse

PIECING ASSEMBLY

- Sew 4 units A-B-C-D.
- Sew 4 units A-B-C-D Reverse.
- Sew ABCD unit to ABCD Reverse unit.
- Sew these 4 units together to complete block.

Template
A

Template
B

Template
C

Template
D & D(R)

FULL-SIZE TEMPLATES
8" BLOCK
Add seam allowances.

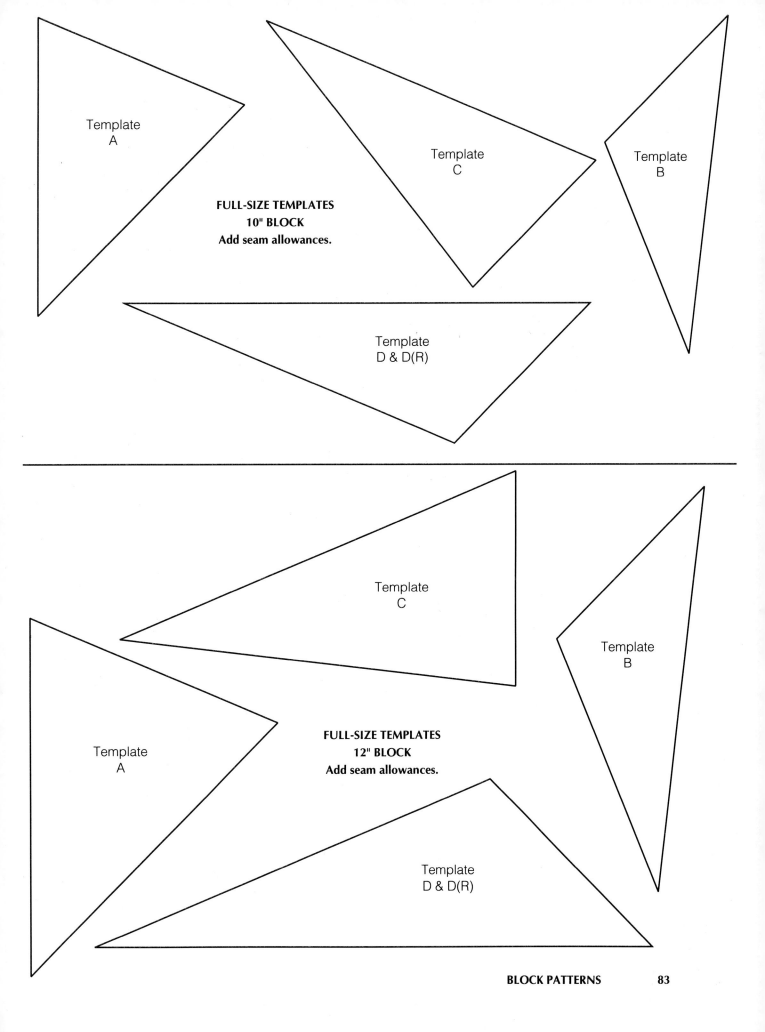

Template
A

Template
C

Template
B

FULL-SIZE TEMPLATES
10" BLOCK
Add seam allowances.

Template
D & D(R)

Template
C

Template
B

Template
A

FULL-SIZE TEMPLATES
12" BLOCK
Add seam allowances.

Template
D & D(R)

SIMPLE STAR

CUT
8A
8B
4C

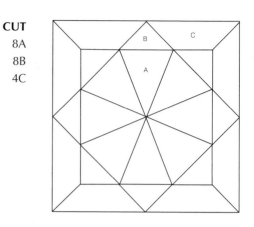

PIECING ASSEMBLY

■ Sew 8 A pieces together to make an octagon.

■ Sew 4 B pieces to the octagon to make a square.

■ Sew 4 units of CBC.

■ Sew CBC units to the square.

■ Sew intersection of C and C units as through it were a mitered border.

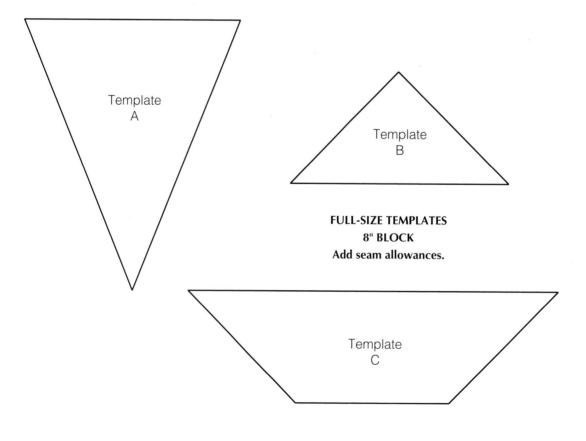

Template
A

Template
B

FULL-SIZE TEMPLATES
8" BLOCK
Add seam allowances.

Template
C

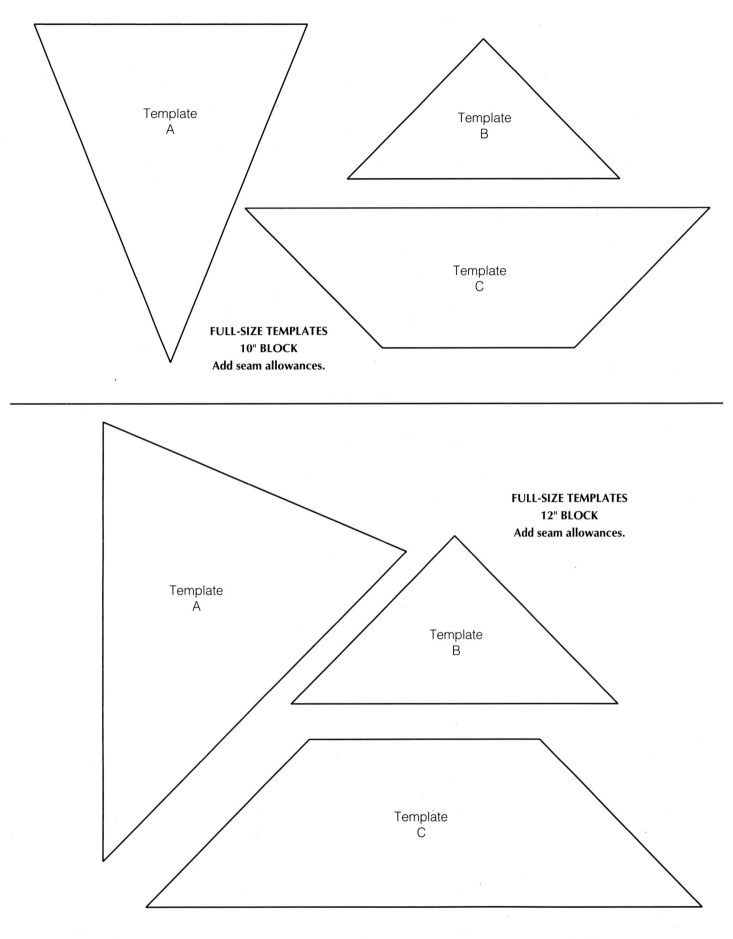

Template
A

Template
B

Template
C

FULL-SIZE TEMPLATES
10" BLOCK
Add seam allowances.

FULL-SIZE TEMPLATES
12" BLOCK
Add seam allowances.

Template
A

Template
B

Template
C

SIX-POINTED STAR

CUT
6 A from chintz
6 A from other material

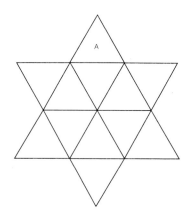

PIECING ASSEMBLY
First Option
- Sew 6 A pieces of chintz together to make a hexagon.
- Sew 6 A other material pieces to outside edges of the hexagon.

Alternative Method
- Sew A chintz piece to A other material piece. Make 6 units.
- Sew units together to make a Six-Pointed Star.
- Sew star to other pieces of your project.

FULL-SIZE TEMPLATE
SMALL STAR
Add seam allowance.

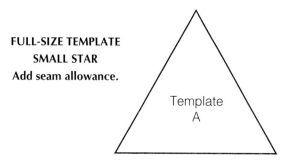

Template
A

FULL-SIZE TEMPLATE
MEDIUM STAR
Add seam allowance.

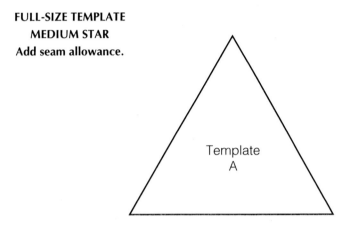

Template
A

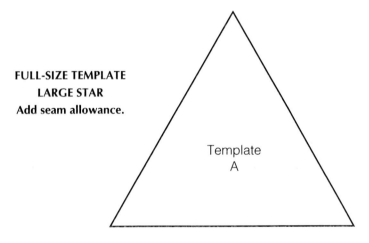

FULL-SIZE TEMPLATE
LARGE STAR
Add seam allowance.

Template
A

WHEEL OF FORTUNE

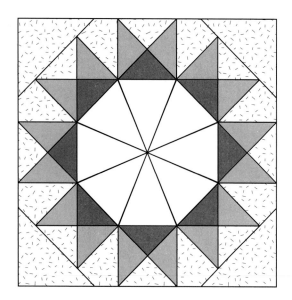

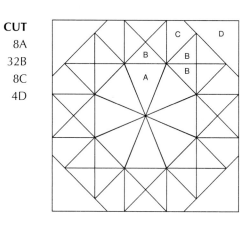

CUT
8A
32B
8C
4D

PIECING ASSEMBLY

- Sew 8 A's together to make an octagon.
- Sew 4 B's to octagon to make a square.
- Sew B-B-B-B units to make 4 squares.
- Sew C-B units. Make 8 units.
- Sew CB units to sides of BBBB units.
- Sew two CB-BBBB units to sides of center unit.
- Sew remaining B units to sides of remaining CB-BBBB units.
- Sew to center unit.
- Sew D triangles to complete block.

FULL-SIZE TEMPLATES
8" BLOCK
Add seam allowances.

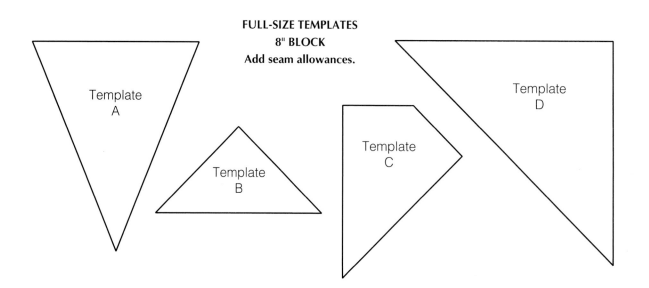

Template A

Template B

Template C

Template D

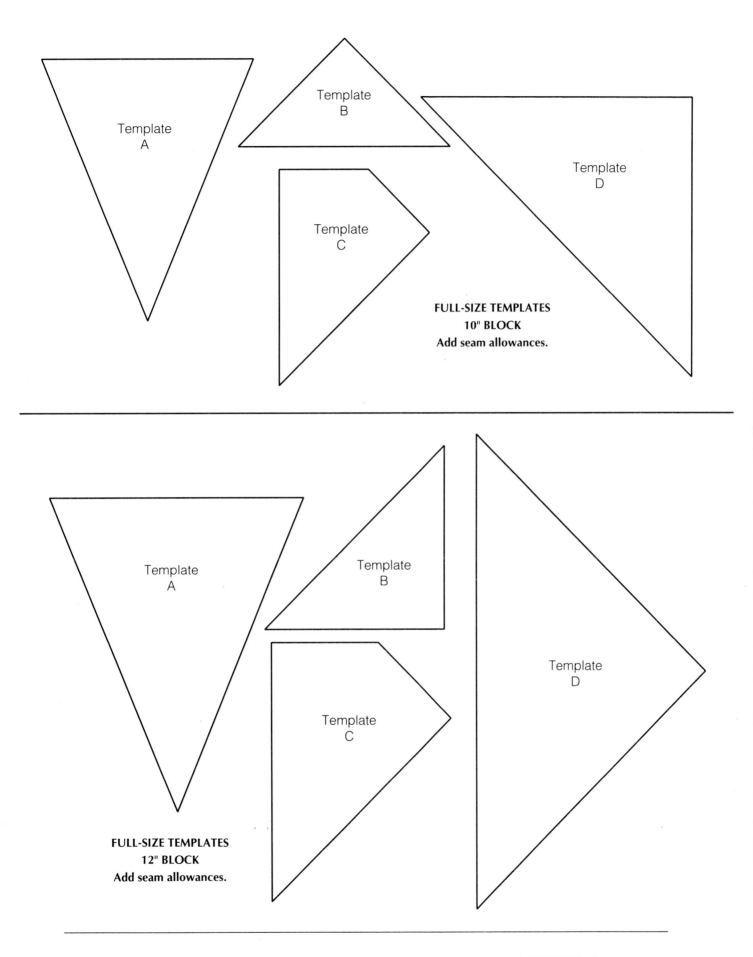

Template
A

Template
B

Template
C

Template
D

FULL-SIZE TEMPLATES
10" BLOCK
Add seam allowances.

Template
A

Template
B

Template
C

Template
D

FULL-SIZE TEMPLATES
12" BLOCK
Add seam allowances.

ANNOTATED REFERENCES

For general instructions on quiltmaking:

Buckley, Karen Kay. *From Basics to Binding: A Complete Guide to Making Quilts.* Paducah, KY: American Quilter's Society, 1992.

Doak, Carol. *Quiltmaker's Guide: Basics and Beyond.* Paducah, KY: American Quilter's Society, 1992.

For instruction about the use of color in quiltmaking:

Wolfrom, J. *The Magical Effects of Color.* Lafayette, CA: C&T Publishing, 1992.

For instruction on drafting quilt blocks:

Beyer, J. *Patchwork Patterns.* McLean, VA: EPM Publications, 1979.

For principles of effective medallion quilt design:

Beyer, J. *Medallion Quilts.* McLean, VA: EPM Publishing, Inc., 1982.

For drafting beautiful feather designs for quilting:

Fons, M. *Fine Feathers.* Lafayette, CA: C&T Publishing, 1988.

Marston, Gwen and Joe Cunningham. *Quilting with Style: Principles for Great Pattern Design.* Paducah, KY: American Quilter's Society, 1993.

For instruction on drafting and making feathered star quilts:

McCloskey, M. *Feathered Star Quilts.* Bothell, WA: That Patchwork Place, 1986.

For general instruction about quilting pieced quilt tops:

Breland, N. "How do you plan to quilt it?" *Quilter's Newsletter Magazine* #243, June, 1992, p. 26-27.

Marston, Gwen and Joe Cunningham. *Quilting with Style: Principles for Great Pattern Design.* Paducah, KY: American Quilter's Society, 1993.

For inspiring geometric designs that can be adapted to quiltmaking: All are available from: Dover Publications, Inc., 31 East 2nd Street, Mineola, NY 11501.

Jones, O. *The Grammar of Ornament.*

Johnston, S. *Mosaic Tile Designs.*

D'Avennes, P. *Arabic Art in Color.*

Hessemer, F. *Historic Designs and Patterns in Color from Arabic and Italian Sources.*

PHOTO CREDITS

Page 3	Jay Turkel	Page 45	Jay Turkel
Page 6	Jay Turkel	Page 46	Jay Turkel
Page 8	Jay Turkel	Page 47	Jay Turkel
Page 13	Charley Lynch	Page 48	Jay Turkel
Page 14	Charley Lynch	Page 49	Jay Turkel
Page 15	Charley Lynch	Page 50	Jay Turkel
Page 16	Charley Lynch	Page 51	Jay Turkel
Page 17	Charley Lynch	Page 52	Jay Turkel
Page 18	Charley Lynch	Page 53	Jay Turkel
Page 19	Jay Turkel	Page 54	Charley Lynch
Page 21	Jay Turkel	Page 55	Charley Lynch
Page 22	Jay Turkel	Page 56	Charley Lynch
Page 23	Jay Turkel	Page 57	Charley Lynch
Page 25	Jay Turkel	Page 58	Charley Lynch
Page 26	Jay Turkel	Page 59	Charley Lynch
Page 27	Jay Turkel		
Page 28	Jay Turkel		
Page 29	Jay Turkel		
Page 30-l	Jay Turkel		
Page 30-r	Jay Turkel		
Page 33-t	Richard Walker		
Page 33-b	Jay Turkel		
Page 35	Jay Turkel		
Page 36	Jay Turkel		
Page 37	Jay Turkel		
Page 42	Jay Turkel		
Page 43	Jay Turkel		
Page 44	Jay Turkel		

INDEX
OF QUILTS

ABOUT
THE AUTHOR

Nancy Breland made her first quilt in 1984 with the help and encouragement of a friend. Since then, her award-winning quilts have appeared in many juried shows throughout the country. Photographs of her quilts and her articles about quilting have appeared in *American Quilter, Quilter's Newsletter Magazine,* and *Quilting Today.*

Nancy received her Ph.D. in Educational Psychology from the State University of New York at Buffalo in 1972. Since then she has been a Professor or Department Chair in the Psychology Department at Trenton State College. She lives with her husband, Hunter, and two daughters, Alison and Julia, in Pennington, New Jersey.

~American Quilter's Society~
dedicated to publishing books for today's quilters

The following AQS publications are currently available:

- **Adapting Architectural Details for Quilts,** Carol Wagner, #2282: AQS, 1991, 88 pages, softbound, $12.95
- **American Beauties: Rose & Tulip Quilts,** Gwen Marston & Joe Cunningham, #1907: AQS, 1988, 96 pages, softbound, $14.95
- **America's Pictorial Quilts,** Caron L. Mosey, #1662: AQS, 1985, 112 pages, hardbound, $19.95
- **Appliqué Designs: My Mother Taught Me to Sew,** Faye Anderson, #2121: AQS, 1990, 80 pages, softbound, $12.95
- **Arkansas Quilts: Arkansas Warmth,** Arkansas Quilter's Guild, Inc., #1908: AQS, 1987, 144 pages, hardbound, $24.95
- **The Art of Hand Applique,** Laura Lee Fritz, #2122: AQS, 1990, 80 pages, softbound, $14.95
- **...Ask Helen: More About Quilting Designs,** Helen Squire, #2099: AQS, 1990, 54 pages, 17 x 11, spiral-bound, $14.95
- **Award-Winning Quilts & Their Makers: Vol. I, The Best of AQS Shows – 1985-1987,** #2207: AQS, 1991, 232 pages, softbound, $24.95
- **Award-Winning Quilts & Their Makers: Vol. II, The Best of AQS Shows – 1988-1989,** #2354: AQS, 1992, 176 pages, softbound, $24.95
- **Award-Winning Quilts & Their Makers: Vol. III, The Best of AQS Shows – 1990-1991,** #3425: AQS, 1993, 180 pages, softbound, $24.95
- **Classic Basket Quilts,** Elizabeth Porter & Marianne Fons, #2208: AQS, 1991, 128 pages, softbound, $16.95
- **A Collection of Favorite Quilts,** Judy Florence, #2119: AQS, 1990, 136 pages, softbound, $18.95
- **Creative Machine Art,** Sharee Dawn Roberts, #2355: AQS, 1992, 142 pages, 9 x 9, softbound, $24.95
- **Dear Helen, Can You Tell Me?...All About Quilting Designs,** Helen Squire, #1820: AQS, 1987, 51 pages, 17 x 11, spiral-bound, $12.95
- **Dye Painting!,** Ann Johnston, #3399: AQS, 1992, 88 pages, softbound, $19.95
- **Dyeing & Overdyeing of Cotton Fabrics,** Judy Mercer Tescher, #2030: AQS, 1990, 54 pages, softbound, $9.95
- **Encyclopedia of Pieced Quilt Patterns,** compiled by Barbara Brackman, #3468: AQS, 1993, 552 pages, hardbound, $34.95
- **Flavor Quilts for Kids to Make: Complete Instructions for Teaching Children to Dye, Decorate & Sew Quilts,** Jennifer Amor #2356: AQS, 1991, 120 pages, softbound, $12.95
- **From Basics to Binding: A Complete Guide to Making Quilts,** Karen Kay Buckley, #2381: AQS, 1992, 160 pages, softbound, $16.95
- **Fun & Fancy Machine Quiltmaking,** Lois Smith, #1982: AQS, 1989, 144 pages, softbound, $19.95
- **Gallery of American Quilts 1830-1991: Book III,** #3421: AQS, 1992, 128 pages, softbound, $19.95
- **The Grand Finale: A Quilter's Guide to Finishing Projects,** Linda Denner, #1924: AQS, 1988, 96 pages, softbound, $14.95
- **Heirloom Miniatures,** Tina M. Gravatt, #2097: AQS, 1990, 64 pages, softbound, $9.95
- **Infinite Stars,** Gayle Bong, #2283: AQS, 1992, 72 pages, softbound, $12.95
- **The Ins and Outs: Perfecting the Quilting Stitch,** Patricia J. Morris, #2120: AQS, 1990, 96 pages, softbound, $9.95
- **Irish Chain Quilts: A Workbook of Irish Chains & Related Patterns,** Joyce B. Peaden, #1906: AQS, 1988, 96 pages, softbound, $14.95
- **Jacobean Appliqué: Book I, "Exotica,"** Patricia B. Campbell & Mini Ayars, Ph.D., #3784: AQS, 1993, 160 pages, softbound, $18.95
- **The Log Cabin Returns to Kentucky: Quilts from the Pilgrim/Roy Collection,** Gerald Roy and Paul Pilgrim, #3329: AQS, 1992, 36 pages, 9 x 7, softbound, $12.95
- **Marbling Fabrics for Quilts: A Guide for Learning & Teaching,** Kathy Fawcett & Carol Shoaf, #2206: AQS, 1991, 72 pages, softbound, $12.95
- **More Projects and Patterns: A Second Collection of Favorite Quilts,** Judy Florence, #3330: AQS, 1992, 152 pages, softbound, $18.95
- **Nancy Crow: Quilts and Influences,** Nancy Crow, #1981: AQS, 1990, 256 pages, 9 x 12, hardcover, $29.95
- **Nancy Crow: Work in Transition,** Nancy Crow, #3331: AQS, 1992, 32 pages, 9 x 10, softbound, $12.95
- **New Jersey Quilts – 1777 to 1950: Contributions to an American Tradition,** The Heritage Quilt Project of New Jersey; text by Rachel Cochran, Rita Erickson, Natalie Hart & Barbara Schaffer, #3332: AQS, 1992, 256 pages, softbound, $29.95
- **No Dragons on My Quilt,** Jean Ray Laury with Ritva Laury & Lizabeth Laury, #2153: AQS, 1990, 52 pages, hardcover, $12.95
- **Oklahoma Heritage Quilts,** Oklahoma Quilt Heritage Project #2032: AQS, 1990, 144 pages, softbound, $19.95
- **Old Favorites in Miniature,** Tina Gravatt #3469: AQS, 1993, 104 pages, softbound, $15.95
- **A Patchwork of Pieces,** compiled by Cuesta Ray Benberry and Carol Pinney Crabb, #3333: AQS, 1993, 360 pages, softbound, $14.95
- **Quilt Groups Today: Who They Are, Where They Meet, What They Do, and How to Contact Them; A Complete Guide for 1992-1993,** #3308: AQS, 1992, 336 pages, softbound, $14.95
- **Quilter's Registry,** Lynne Fritz, #2380: AQS, 1992, 80 pages, hardbound, $9.95
- **Quilting Patterns from Native American Designs,** Dr. Joyce Mori, #3467: AQS, 1993, 80 pages, softbound, $12.95
- **Quilting with Style: Principles for Great Pattern Design,** Gwen Marston & Joe Cunningham #3470: AQS, 1993, 192 pages, 9 x 12, hardbound, $24.95
- **Quiltmaker's Guide: Basics & Beyond,** Carol Doak, #2284: AQS, 1992, 208 pages, softbound, $19.95
- **Quilts: Old & New, A Similar View,** Paul D. Pilgrim and Gerald E. Roy, #3715: AQS, 1993, 40 pages, softbound, $12.95
- **Quilts: The Permanent Collection – MAQS,** #2257: AQS, 1991, 100 pages, 10 x 6½, softbound, $9.95
- **Seasons of the Heart & Home: Quilts for a Winter's Day,** Jan Patek, #3796: AQS, 1993, 160 pages, softbound, $18.95
- **Seasons of the Heart & Home: Quilts for Summer Days,** Jan Patek, #3761: AQS, 1993, 160 pages, softbound, $18.95
- **Sensational Scrap Quilts,** Darra Duffy Williamson, #2357: AQS, 1992, 152 pages, softbound, $24.95
- **Sets & Borders,** Gwen Marston & Joe Cunningham, #1821: AQS, 1987, 104 pages, softbound, $14.95
- **Show Me Helen...How to Use Quilting Designs,** Helen Squire, #3375: AQS, 1993, 155 pages, softbound, $15.95
- **Somewhere in Between: Quilts and Quilters of Illinois,** Rita Barrow Barber, #1790: AQS, 1986, 78 pages, softbound, $14.95
- **Spike & Zola: Patterns Designed for Laughter ... and Appliqué, Painting or Stenciling,** Donna French Collins, #3794: AQS, 1993, 72 pages, soft bound, $9.95
- **Stenciled Quilts for Christmas,** Marie Monteith Sturmer, #2098: AQS, 1990, 104 pages, softbound, $14.95
- **A Treasury of Quilting Designs,** Linda Goodmon Emery, #2029: AQS, 1990, 80 pages, 14 x 11, spiral-bound, $14.95
- **Wonderful Wearables: A Celebration of Creative Clothing,** Virginia Avery, #2286: AQS, 1991, 184 pages, softbound, $24.95

These books can be found in local bookstores and quilt shops. If you are unable to locate a title in your area, you can order by mail from AQS, P.O. Box 3290, Paducah, KY 42002-3290.
Please add $1 for the first book and 40¢ for each additional one to cover postage and handling.
(International orders please add $1.50 for the first book and $1 for each additional one.)